Neglected Children and Their Families

Neglected Children and Their Families

Second Edition

Olive Stevenson

Olive Stevenson, CBE, D.Litt, MA (Oxon) is Professor Emeritus at Nottingham University, where she has a continuing contract to teach and supervise research. She holds honorary degrees from the Universities of East Anglia and Kingston. She is an honorary professor at the University of Kingston and the Poly-University of Hong Kong.

Blackwell
Publishing

© 2007 by Olive Stevenson.

Blackwell Publishing editorial offices:
Blackwell Publishing Ltd, 9600 Garsington Road, Oxford OX4 2DQ, UK
Tel: +44 (0)1865 776868
Blackwell Publishing Inc., 350 Main Street, Malden, MA 02148-5020, USA
Tel: +1 781 388 8250
Blackwell Publishing Asia Pty Ltd, 550 Swanston Street, Carlton, Victoria
3053, Australia
Tel: +61 (0)3 8359 1011

First published 2007 by Blackwell Publishing Ltd

ISBN: 978-1-4051-5171-9

Library of Congress Cataloging-in-Publication Data

Stevenson, Olive.
Neglected children and their families / Olive Stevenson. – 2nd ed.
p.   cm.
Includes bibliographical references and index.
ISBN-13: 978-1-4051-5171-9 (pbk. : alk. paper)
ISBN-10: 1-4051-5171-4 (pbk. : alk. paper)
1. Child welfare–Great Britain.   2. Family social work–Great
Britain.   I. Title.
HV751.A6S67 2007
362.760941–dc22
2006102873

A catalogue record for this title is available from the British Library

Set in 10/12 pt Palatino
by SNP Best-set Typesetter Ltd., Hong Kong
Printed and bound in Singapore
by COS Printers Pte Ltd

The publisher's policy is to use permanent paper from mills that operate
a sustainable forestry policy, and which has been manufactured from
pulp processed using acid-free and elementary chlorine-free practices.
Furthermore, the publisher ensures that the text paper and cover board
used have met acceptable environmental accreditation standards.

For further information on Blackwell Publishing, visit our website:
www.blackwellpublishing.com

To the memory of my parents who cherished me

Contents

Update to First Edition Foreword

This book should be of interest and relevance to practitioners and policy makers alike whose interest is working to prevent and effectively intervene in families where children are neglected. Not only does it comprehensively review the literature and research on neglect, it also has very practical application. It provides the reader with evidence from practice of what works when seeking to improve outcomes for this group of children.

Seeking first to understand the historical, social, economic, and parenting factors in children who are neglected, and then those less commonly dwelt upon, such as mothers' health and drugs abuse, the book draws the reader's attention to the importance of valued thorough assessment and planning to build on strengths and to meet children's timescales.

This book has been comprehensively updated to draw on very social and economic realities and policy context of 2007. These are quite different to those obtained in the late 1990s, at least in their aspirations for the eradication of poverty and the inclusion of all our citizens and the vital importance of social cohesion.

Any social worker, health visitor, police officer, teacher or community paediatrician will recognise the portrait of children who are neglected and will recognise the devastating impact of neglect on healthy development. What has not changed over recent years is that this cohort of children provides the most intractable of dilemmas for practice and management and are the most telling representation of the effects of social exclusion and poverty. Olive Stevenson has at one and the same time addressed these wider strategic economic issues, and also provided an analysis for practice, which is no mean feat.

When I first wrote the foreword to this book in 1998, I wrote from the perspective of an Executive Director of Social Services in a large northern city who had herself worked up from being a social worker in the 1970s and could identify with many of the characteristics of families portrayed in this book. I reflected on how useful this book would have been for me when I was in practice, and I recommended it to practitioners who are now working in the field.

In commending the book, I drew attention to the hard work and dedication of practitioners and policy makers whose work on assessment and planning in the 1990s had contributed significantly to making an impact on improving the well being of children and young people. I was an Executive Director of Social Services seeking to support the use of research in every day work, and to champion partnership working in a very meaningful and practical way as the only means of tackling the distress of individual children and their families when neglect was evident. I commended the book hoping that it would help my staff and those across the country to develop confidence to be assertive practitioners putting the interest of children at the forefront and recognising that a cycle of disadvantage if not broken has lasting and devastating consequences.

I now write this foreword as a Chief Executive of an inner London borough all of whose wards are in the most deprived of those in the country. A borough of contrast where well off, successful inhabitants, benefiting from the prosperity of London, live cheek by jowl with some of the most impoverished of our citizens, many of whom have come to this country to find refuge from war or natural disaster seeking to improve conditions for themselves and opportunities for their children. And you might ask why a local authority Chief Executive would want to be interested in research and practice regarding neglect. The reason is simple. The agenda for local authorities is to provide community leadership and 'place shaping'; to promote the well being of citizens in its area. Recognising and tackling the neglect of our most vulnerable children has got to be at the heart of this agenda. One of the effects of local government legislation and children's legislation in recent years has been to bring the agenda for well being, regeneration and safeguarding to the heart of local government, and very much into the main stream agenda for local authority Chief Executives. Because of this, I commend Olive's book and its recent updating and hope that it can play a part in assisting those who work on our behalf with these most intractable difficulties to be able to do so with an increased effectiveness. Whilst we champion an agenda that puts the five outcomes for all children at the heart of our arrangements, we cannot afford to ourselves neglect the most hard to reach, and difficult to work with, families where children's most basic needs are not being met. Research has highlighted the importance of early years parenting on later outcomes and this book reinforces that message.

Penny Thompson
Chief Executive
London Borough of Hackney

Foreword to Second Edition

This is a very timely point at which to publish this new edition. Inevitably I have looked at it through the spectacles of a social worker trained in the early 1970s and, as I am now, a strategic director of children's services currently charged with the responsibility to support local authorities across England in the establishment of children's centres.

I come from a generation of social workers whose reading list certainly included the names of experts about whom Olive Stevenson reminds us in this book; experts who wrote about the essentials for healthy child development and the observable consequences for children when their parenting was 'not good enough'. In those days the observation of children and the impact of their experiences on their development was a focal point for social work. Olive reminds us about the huge body of evidence that exists about the impact of neglect on every aspect of a child's well-being – their health, their ability to learn and their own future parenting skills. However, she also reminds us about why some of these issues are so intractable.

The book brings these perspectives back into play in the context of the current policy environment for children's services and the issues in family life that have increasingly impacted on children over the decade since the first edition. The outcomes for the children of seriously neglectful parents are very poor indeed and the search for interventions that address this remains as challenging as ever. There are huge questions about whether the introduction of a universally available early years service based on a national network of children's centres will make a difference to what Olive calls 'our' children. These are the children, and their families, whose characteristics are described in this book. They exist on the margins of mainstream society, often 'disorganised', often 'depressed' and rarely amenable to simple instruction on how to improve their lives.

There is already much evidence of the benefits derived from the precursors of children's centres (the Sure Start Local Programmes) but as Olive points out, we face a very challenging task if these benefits are to reach children whose lives are blighted by the most extreme forms of chronic neglect.

This task challenges all involved in children's services within the newly integrated environments that are being created by local authorities and their partners. This book will not only be of interest to the many social workers who continue to hold Olive Stevenson in the highest regard but also to teachers, health professionals and the new generation of children's centre managers for whom improving the lives of neglected children will be a key challenge. There is a core base of knowledge and skills to which Olive refers in this book that needs to be held in common by everyone who works in children's services.

Liz Railton CBE
Programme Director
Together for Children

Preface

Those who work with seriously neglectful families will recognise this description. Paula Simmons, who is twenty-five, has three children, Alan aged eight, Mary three and Kevin eighteen months. The children have different fathers and there is no man currently living in the household. Paula has been known to social services since she was a child; she was in care for short periods and was known to be neglected as a child, and sexually abused in her teens by her stepfather.

There is serious concern about Paula's capacity to offer adequate care to the children. Alan is already known as a budding delinquent in the neighbourhood. His school attendance is erratic and he has been excluded for indiscipline several times. He is teased and bullied by his peers because of his poor clothing and unkempt appearance. He is below average in attainment. Paula cannot offer him effective control and he is often out late in the evening. He is a healthy boy of average intelligence, but seems an angry child and shows little warmth to his mother.

Mary seems a rather miserable child. She attends a family centre and frequently arrives smelly and seemingly hungry, often with a runny nose and a skin rash. Her general development, physical and intellectual, is delayed and she has a marked squint. There has been concern that she has not been taken to hospital appointments about this. She constantly seeks affection and reassurance and is very jealous of younger children.

Kevin was a premature baby and was a very difficult baby to feed. He is very passive. During infancy, there was doubt as to whether he was appropriately stimulated.

Paula takes little care of her appearance and often appears tired, dispirited and 'flat', with little interest in responding to the children. She struggles to manage financially and is in debt to 'loan sharks' in the area. She is not well physically, often complaining of heavy periods, but is frightened of going to the doctor, in case 'something bad' is found to be the matter. She welcomes visits from health visitors and social workers and will talk at length about the many difficulties which she encounters. She struggles to keep up with the housework and there are times when standards get worryingly low, with flea infestation, unwashed crockery and clothes, and a very dirty toilet. Her own personal hygiene is poor.

Those who visit become fond of her. They see a woman who is struggling to survive in very difficult circumstances and who needs much support. However, the quality of life for the children does not seem acceptable, no matter what efforts are made to help. They are not receiving 'good enough' physical care, supervision, control and warmth to ensure their proper development. Health visitors and social workers have put a lot of time and energy, with a range of services, into this family. But now they are anxious and uncertain what to do.

Since the first edition of this book was published in 1998, there have been many changes in law, policy and practice in children's services. There has also been new research which has strengthened the evidence of the adverse effects of neglect on children's development. There is also evidence that increasing numbers of children have been placed on the Child Protection Register for neglect, but little indication that practice in this area has improved to any significant extent.

The preparation of this edition has coincided with public anxiety about 'antisocial' children and young people. 'Social exclusion' is an issue which has received much attention from the present government, but the Prime Minister (Blair, 2006) has acknowledged that there is a group of families and children which has not responded to the support offered and for which other measures are necessary.

Seriously neglected children, who are the focus of this book, undoubtedly form part of this socially excluded group but it is not clear how far the analysis of their family life given here can be applied more generally. How far is the neglectful parenting at the root of the children's bad behaviour? How far is it part of more general maltreatment, not just neglect? (We know that serious neglect is often associated with other forms of abuse.) How far are we seeing much wider social problems in contemporary society for which individualised interventions are simply inadequate?

These are questions which I cannot answer. What is indisputable is that poor parental control and supervision of children is almost always a feature of seriously neglected children. It is essential that this aspect of neglect is taken as seriously as its other familiar manifestations, such as poor nutrition and hygiene.

Acknowledgements

I am indebted to many more people and to a far greater extent than is customary for an author. Because this book attempts to bring together material from a wide variety of sources, both from literature and from the professional and academic experience of friends and colleagues, I have unashamedly begged and borrowed (but not, I hope, stolen) from many people, not all of whom I can name here. My thanks to them is no less warm, including those whose work forms an important part of the appendices.

In the preparation of the second edition, I have particularly appreciated the prompt responses of those whom I have urgently asked for advice. Special thanks to Jonathan Dickens for his help over legal issues.

Despite the miracles of modern technology, I would have been lost without the invaluable support of Julie Ball, who has patiently dealt with my incompetence. Her high standards of accuracy have made the preparation of this second edition much less onerous.

Defining and Understanding the Problem

Introduction

Since the introduction to the 1998 edition was written, my concern (or burden as I described it then) about the plight of neglected children and their families has increased. Others share this concern; there has been a considerable body of thoughtful research and reflection on the topic. Now, as in 1998, professionals agree that neglect as an aspect of child abuse is not at present satisfactorily handled by British child protection services; many also know that there is quite strong evidence that the longer-term effects of neglect on children may be even more serious than sporadic physical injury as a result of abuse. Yet, somehow, the nettle has not been grasped. Assessment and protection plans have been less effective than for physical abuse. It is widely acknowledged that professionals may feel a sense of relief when there is an 'incident' or a 'happening' in a particular family (whether of sexual or physical abuse), which is seen to legitimate action for children about whom neglect has long been a primary concern. In what follows, I shall discuss the reasons for the difficulties, both professional and academic, in addressing the issue and make some suggestions of ways forward.

This introductory chapter identifies problems. Much of the rest of the book explores these problems in greater depth. For this reason, I have largely avoided the rather irritating authors' habit of referring the reader to later chapters.

The evidence that there are grounds for serious anxiety about the position of seriously neglected children is to be found in statistics, in Serious Case Reviews and in the reported experience of practitioners. The records of the three years, 2001–2004, show that the proportion of children registered for the category of neglect was far higher than the other categories. They have been constant at 41% for neglect, 19% for physical abuse, 18% for emotional abuse and 9% for sexual abuse (mixed categories, in which neglect features, make up the rest). Decisions to place children on the Child Protection Register are taken with reluctance and, therefore, for example, it can be assumed that, in 2004, more than 11 000 children in England and Wales were seriously neglected (DfES, 2005a).

The most extreme consequences of neglect are to be found in Serious Case Reviews. Most of those who participated in area child protection committees (not then local safeguarding children's boards) are familiar with such tragic cases where children have died or there have been 'near misses'. In 1995 we were shocked by the story of the death of 'Paul' in Islington; the inquiry report revealed both the inadequacies of family care and of the services designed to support it (The Bridge Consultancy, 1995). Yet, in 2005, a report on a family in Sheffield in which two children missed death by a matter of hours or days, revealed similar inadequacies (Cantrill, 2005). What has been learnt (or not learnt) in these ten years?

The practitioners' view is usually bleak, even when dealing with cases which do not arouse fears of death or near death. We shall examine later the feelings which such families arouse in those who work closely with them; confusion and despair loom large. Those reading this book who work, in whatever capacity, with such families and their children, will have no trouble in conjuring up in their minds the children of whom I am writing. Perhaps these mental pictures will help to keep us focused as complex issues are addressed. I remember speaking to a middle-aged woman who told me how vividly she recalled, at the age of five, the little classmate who always arrived at school smelly and with dirty knickers. 'The first thing the class teacher did was to give her a wash and clean knickers.' To me, the striking thing was that the memory was so fresh, showing the impact that one child, somehow 'different', made on other children. Neglect is not, of course, only about physical and external well-being. But the example reminds us that in the families we shall be considering there is usually a sense of social distance from others and an awareness of difference, which in turn provokes reactions in the family members and the community within which they are located: in truth, a vicious circle.

Furthermore, evidence accumulates of the long-standing, even permanent, damage which serious neglect inflicts on children: Tanner and

Turney (2006, p. 1) in reviewing the evidence, point out that 'research highlights the deleterious effects of neglect, in its own right, in children's development and challenges a common perception that it is ancillary to "more serious" forms of abuse, such as physical or sexual abuse.'

Definitions: arguments and limitations

This book is focused on serious and sustained neglect of children which affects various aspects of their development. It is not about ordinary parents who, from time to time, omit to care adequately in some respects, not even about those who show emerging signs of neglectful parenthood. The cases we consider are found at the end of a continuum. Indicators of trouble ahead are often observable at early stages in the life of a family. This raises important questions about early detection and remedial 'preventative' work.

The government in power since 1997 has placed considerable emphasis on family support, with a variety of initiatives of which Sure Start has been particularly prominent. These schemes, designed to assist parents and young children in a range of ways, have been developed and evaluated over several years. Although the focus of this book is on families who are already in serious difficulties, there is obviously an issue as to whether earlier intervention could have effected change.

The affirmation of the importance of family support and of provision to children in need offers a positive approach to intervening constructively with families in difficulties and is particularly relevant to cases of potential or developing neglect. Indeed, in policy terms, there is a case for concentrating effort in that sphere, since, as we shall see, the evidence for success in intervention when there is serious neglect is shaky. Nonetheless, the moral and economic arguments for improving the quality of help offered to seriously neglectful families are unassailable. Although the emphasis of the present policy has great merit, there is a danger that less concentration on the complex and intractable aspects of child protection work may lead to yet further 'neglect of serious neglect'. Such cases are small in number but in terms of human misery, professional time and energy, long-term damage and long-term costs, their significance is disproportionate.

The definition of neglect used in this book largely corresponds to that of the latest guidance in *Working Together* (DfES, 2006). Definitions of neglect are controversial. This is illustrated well by Zuravin (Dubowitz, 1999). However, I have taken the view that, for the purposes of this book, which is focused on serious neglect, there can be a workable consensus, such as that offered in this recent DfES guidance.

'1.33 Neglect is the *persistent* failure to meet a child's basic physical and/or psychological needs, likely to result in the *serious* impairment of the child's health or development. Neglect may occur during pregnancy as a result of maternal substance abuse. Once a child is born, neglect may involve a parent or carer failing to provide adequate food or clothing, shelter including exclusion from home or abandonment, failing to protect a child from physical or emotional harm or danger, failure to ensure adequate supervision including the use of inadequate caretakers, or the failure to ensure access to appropriate medical care or treatment. It may also include neglect of, or unresponsiveness to, a child's basic emotional needs.' (DfES, 2006) (my italics)

This definition is more detailed and sophisticated than in earlier guidance (see, for example, DoH, 1989). The reference to neglect in pregnancy is particularly valuable. It makes clear the various forms which neglect of children can take. Broadly, it covers the areas critical to healthy development: physical, psychological and social. However, within the term 'psychological' there are two components, cognitive and emotional, and it is disappointing that these are not referred to specifically in this definition, although these matters are acknowledged in subsequent discussion.

'9.10 Severe neglect of young children has adverse effects on children's ability to form attachments and is associated with major impairment of growth and intellectual development. Persistent neglect can lead to serious impairment of health and development, and long-term difficulties with social functioning, relationships and educational progress. Neglected children may also experience low self-esteem, feelings of being unloved and isolated. Neglect can also result, in extreme cases, in death. The impact of neglect varies depending on how long children have been neglected, the children's age, and the multiplicity of neglectful behaviours children have been experiencing.' (DfES, 2006)

In recent years, there have been major advances in our understanding of the development of the brain in infancy and early childhood. This throws more light on the long-term effects of neglect, in particular, of under stimulation, on children's development. As for 'emotional' neglect, a holistic model of child development, surely now uncontroversial, carries with it the assumption that all 'persistent failure' to meet developmental needs is inherently emotionally harmful.

Research undertaken by Glaser *et al.* confirms the importance of keeping these two aspects of maltreatment, neglect and emotional abuse, linked in the minds of those in child protection work (Glaser *et al.*, 1997). They investigated 94 children from 56 families; 54% of these children were registered under the sole category of emotional abuse and 48% were registered jointly for emotional abuse and one or more categories of abuse or neglect. The mean age of the children at registration was seven years five months, but nearly all had been known to social services departments for varying lengths of time, some substantial. Most of the forms of ill-treatment to which the children had been subjected are highly significant in relation to consideration of neglect; for example 27% were found to have been emotionally abused through 'emotional unavailability or neglect', 34% through 'denigration or rejection' and 42% through 'developmentally inappropriate interaction with the child'.

The more one probes the definitions and distinctions between emotional abuse and neglect the less satisfactory they become. When neglect is construed as an omission of care, which affects not only physical but social, intellectual and emotional development, the association between the two becomes clear. For example, if an infant is said to have 'dirtied his nappy on purpose' and is left unchanged, this may be due to 'developmentally inappropriate' expectations but it leads to neglect of physical care. If a six-year-old is required to undertake tasks (or roles) for which he/she is too young and adult/child boundaries are blurred, this may lead to neglect of his/her social, intellectual and emotional needs as a six-year-old (for play, cuddles, etc.). We may well have reached a stage when clarification and reshaping of these categories are appropriate. Meanwhile, however, whatever the wider ramifications, there is much work to be done to address more systematically those aspects of maltreatment in which omission of care places well-being and development in jeopardy.

One important issue, discussed at some length, which arises in any discussion of the nature of neglect or emotional abuse, is the significance of cultural factors in the definition of the problem. Whilst in no way minimising the intrinsic interest and importance of cultural factors in approaching families where neglect is the subject of concern, such debates should not divert us from a recognition that there is a very significant cross-cultural consensus about the basic needs for healthy child development. To the extent that cultural factors are 'a problem' in addressing neglect, it may be as much about the approach and anxieties of workers as about the definition of serious neglect itself.

Although current literature and guidance accepts the significance of neglect, which goes beyond the grosser and more obvious manifestations of physical and hygienic deficiencies, it is sadly evident that in cases which 'hit the headlines', these draw the more attention. It may be that some of the workers involved are less sensitive to the other elements or are, perhaps, worried that only these long-standing and familiar indicators will be convincing to seniors or to lawyers.

Here it is argued that it is equally important to examine the parents' ability to protect their children from physical and emotional hazards and from untreated medical conditions. Furthermore, the reference to lack of 'appropriate supervision' means much more than the occasional 'left alone in the house' incident. There is a very real danger, which I have discussed elsewhere (Stevenson, 1996) that, if multiple minor 'accidents' cannot be conclusively established as intentional abuse, they are discounted, whereas they may be indicative of quite inadequate parental supervision or abuse, both of which must be taken seriously. This was graphically illustrated in the inquiry into the death of Stephanie Fox (Lynch & Stevenson, 1990) in which a total of 27 minor injuries, many to the head, were recorded to Stephanie and her siblings in the last two years of her life, and the number increased markedly in the last six months of her life. Argument concerning parental 'intention' may simply deflect us from effective appraisal of the parents' ability to provide a safe enough environment for the child.

Neglect, then, covers a wide range of behaviours. We do not seek a 'neglectful parents' syndrome', within which understanding can be conveniently packaged, although there are certain aspects of neglectful behaviour and children's responses (such as attachment theory) which can be helpfully viewed from particular theoretical perspectives. Crittenden (1999) proposed a model for differentiating different types of neglectful parenting. She argues that a socio-economic explanation is not adequate to explain it and suggests an analysis based on 'distortions of mental processing' (p. 47). Three categories of neglect are considered, 'disorganised', 'emotionally neglecting' and 'depressed'. (See Chapter 5.) Crittenden herself is tentative about the validity of many of the propositions made, acknowledging that there is insufficient evidence to confirm them. However, she argues, convincingly, that 'the dual perspectives of individual pathology and societal failure have not led to effective solutions to the problem of neglect' (p. 67). Whether or not this model is accepted, its strength lies in the attempt to distinguish between kinds of parental difficulty which lead to neglect. It offers workers an opportunity to find alternative ways of understanding and helping the families when they seek to help.

'Thresholds'

The word 'threshold' has been frequently used in the debates about neglect amongst practitioners and managers. It is a kind of professional shorthand, reflecting some of the anxiety and confusion surrounding intervention in such cases. The only relevant definition in the *Oxford English Dictionary* is 'entrance'. Entrance to what, one may ask? The term is now used much more often in relation to neglect than other categories of maltreatment. It can be described as 'movement to the next phase' of intervention, but it also carries the connotation of a 'gateway, a distinguishable step, not simply movement on a continuum'. Until the publication of the latest *Working Together* (DoH, 2006) there were three key thresholds in the assessment of neglect, in each of which the judgements were made on children's well-being and parental capacity. These were: to categorise a neglected child as in need of services; to place the child on the Child Protection Register; to go to the courts, which might result in the removal of the child. (Following the recommendations of the Victoria Climbié enquiry (2003), the decision has been taken to abolish the Child Protection Register.) The Department of Health (1995), in *Messages for Research*, devoted a section of the guidance (pp. 14–18) to discussion of the concepts of thresholds.

It is interesting that there are few references to thresholds in the latest guidance (DfES, 2006); nor indeed was the term significant in the earlier guidance of 2000 (DoH, 2000). What these documents stress is an orderly path from referral onwards, with defined steps, set out in great detail. They are based on the now familiar 'triangle' for assessment (see Appendix 5) upon which judgements are to be made, and suggest the possibility of a seamless process, in which the significance of particular thresholds will be less important. However that may be, there will, inevitably, be a threshold at the point when consideration is given to the removal of a child. Furthermore, the vital question (is the child, or the care he or she is receiving, getting better or worse?) requires appraisals which may mark critical turning points in the lives of the families. For many, the word threshold suggested the value of measurement, a need for accuracy and precision in the making of these grave decisions. It is a short step from this to questionnaires, checklists and forms. Yet, many workers at field level, not least in the field of child protection, resent such growing trends. Since the first edition of this book, workers have been operating within the *Framework for the Assessment of Children in Need and their Families* (DoH, 2000), which provides very detailed guidance (2000a; b) and a variety of scales and checklists (2000c). The triangle itself is particularly helpful in relation to neglected children and their families. The scales and checklists, which refer to maltreatment generally, are much less useful if the focus is on serious neglect. It may be that some more work, especially on measures of children's well-being, will prove useful. However, the underlying problem, epitomised by the longing for clear thresholds, has to be accepted by practitioners and is, indeed, implicit in the guidance now offered. There will never be automated processes by which these grave decisions can be made. It is high time that the workers involved (and the managers and lawyers who advise them) marshal the well-founded evidence from many sources now available to make the necessary judgements. 'Waiting for an incident' should be a thing of the past.

Wider factors

This chapter is entitled 'Defining and Understanding the Problem'. So far, the discussion has focused on the notion of neglect as a category of maltreatment. But the failure to tackle the problem adequately goes further and is, in some ways, deeper than these conceptual and procedural difficulties. It would be naive, therefore, to hope for significant improvement in work with neglectful families without seeking to understand and hence to modify some of the existing contextual difficulties.

In common with other work with people in difficulty, there is confusion and fear at the heart of this debate. The injunction to 'condemn the sin and not the sinner' has been at the centre of the ethical framework for social work for many years. It is, of course, extremely difficult to preserve this distinction. There is a deep-rooted feeling that by attributing difficulties, in part at least, to the behaviour of the person concerned, one is blaming them. There is, of course, a way round that, if it can be shown that the difficulties (for example in parenting) may be connected to earlier experiences (for example in childhood) over which the parent had no control, or indeed, to basic limitations in ability. Yet that, in turn, leads to increased concern about a model for understanding which appears to diminish personal responsibility. It is felt that it is a slippery slope and may encourage dependence, instead of building on strengths. Part of the fear of 'blaming' reflects a legitimate concern that individualistic explanations of deviant behaviour may be used to deflect attention from social deficits and social evils. This is often presented as a dichotomy between the left and the right politically. But this places the professionals in an untenable position. They should not have to deny or inhibit their insight into the difficulties of parents for fear of being 'aligned' with the right of politics.

A particular difficulty in working with neglect has arisen from what has been described as the 'forensic model' in investigation of child maltreatment. This has led to the emphasis on incidents and episodes to which I have earlier referred, rather than on a more holistic approach. This shift has been referred to in terms of 'socio-legal' rather than 'socio-medical' discourse. The former, although it has its place in the range of activities in child abuse investigations, can have a curiously blocking effect on the search for understanding which must precede long-term judgements about intervention. Short-term decisions may indeed have to be made simply on 'happenings' which place a child at risk. But when we enter the field of intelligent anticipation (not prediction) and the likelihood of future harm is considered, the need for the holistic approach is demonstrable and essential in cases of neglect. However, the term 'socio-medical' needs qualification, for it carries with it the baggage of past conflict in the field of child abuse and elsewhere. For a start, it raised fears of domination by two, differing but narrow, approaches which have been influential and controversial. The first, ironically, supported a socio-legal or forensic way of looking at the problem, for it sought to establish precision and reliability in diagnosis. No one can doubt its value given the early resistance of the medical profession to the belief in the existence of 'battered' babies and its utility within the judicial system itself, but its limitations have become increasingly apparent, especially in relation to neglect.

The second approach, epitomised in the work of Kempe (for example Kempe & Helfer, 1968) stressed mental health problems of the parents in the aetiology of child abuse. Again, this has played, and will continue to play, an important part in raising awareness of such connections. But it has also been sharply criticised because of the biased samples on which early studies were based and because the very use of certain psychiatric and psychoanalytic classifications is controversial. The consequences of this approach may, it has been argued, lead to altogether too pessimistic a view of the characteristics of those who abuse their children. Yet whatever terminology we use, and there are difficulties associated with alternatives, we need a phrase to express the holistic ideal which is at the heart of effective and purposeful thought about abusive parents, most particularly neglectful ones. It seems likely, then, that workers have been caught in a kind of pincer movement: from one side, guilt and anxiety about 'blaming' and unease about the use of 'pathological' descriptors; from the other, an organisational context which has discouraged systematic reflection about people, rather than events.

A further difficulty concerns the courts and the judicial process. Work with neglected children and their families often starts well before the involvement of the courts and may never reach them. More effective work with 'children in need' may further reduce the need for courts to be brought into the process. However, it is evident, from what social workers have said, that the shadow of the courts hangs unhelpfully over their heads when they are confronting serious cases of neglect. This centres on the nature of evidence needed for neglect to be proved. In some ways, this is surprising. Workers are extremely unlikely to take cases to court without grounds for serious concern. There is now an accepted corpus of literature on children's physical, intellectual and emotional needs; it is unlikely that magistrates and judges would be reluctant to make orders on the basis of definite and systematically collected evidence. However, it is apparent that these tensions between social workers and those involved in the judicial process, including local authority lawyers, still present major obstacles in the management of cases of neglect (Iwaniec *et al.*, 2004; Dickens, 2006). (See Chapter 5.)

Whatever the part played by the courts, everyone concerned is aware that, in many cases (though not all), failure to provide good enough care by parents is bound up with their limitations in ability, distressing family backgrounds and mental health problems. When chronic poverty is added to this, there may be a pervasive sense of sympathy, linked to the hope that such parents can be helped to improve their care sufficiently to permit the children to stay at home. The lack of precision concerning the effects of neglect on development plays into the chronic indecision which is so often a feature of work in such cases. Optimism about the potentiality for change must, however, be under-pinned by realism, by a reasonable knowledge base about likely and unlikely change and improvement in parenting capacity and the conditions necessary for it. On this matter there is research, mainly from the USA, which offers some valuable insights, discussed later. Nonetheless, when critical discussions concerning the future of the children have to be taken, and the courts are bound to consider the capacity of parents to sustain or improve the existing quality of care, we are in foggier territory than in relation to child development. The imperative that we should seek to work in partnership with parents, linked to uncertainty as to what change or development is possible, has led to some decisions to leave children at home whose quality of life is simply not good enough.

However, uncertainties and anxieties surrounding work with neglectful families are also affected by its organisational context. The shift from 'socio-medical' to 'socio-legal' approaches has been funda-mentally unhelpful in cases of neglect because it can cause the wrong or less important question to be asked. Many professionals are enthu-siastic about a shift of paradigm, a different way of looking at abuse, which will encompass neglect more satisfactorily. Tanner and Turney (2003) have stressed the importance of sustained work, 'to be based on clear assessment, objectives for change, strategies for achieving change and a way of evaluating whether change has taken place' (p. 32). They coin the phrase 'managed dependency' to describe a method of working in which the worker is not trapped in an unhelpful dependency rela-tionship but uses it in a purposeful way to achieve change in parental attitudes and behaviour.

There has been little indication that those who manage social ser-vices for children have recognised the need for long-term support for some neglectful families. Indeed, the culture has been in various ways inimical to such practice. Targets were set which placed value on cases closed, being taken off the register of protected children or re-registered. Thus, there were perverse incentives against prolonged and systematic work with certain families. (The abolition of the register will, of course, have a bearing on this.) There needs to be an explicit acceptance that, for a small number of families, long-term work is the only realistic, morally justifiable alternative to removal of the children.

There are two further matters of great significance in understanding the nature of the problem which confronts us. The first concerns the sympathy and compassion which some parents (usually mothers) of neglected children raise in workers, especially health visitors and social workers. So often the parents have themselves been the victims of the same type of upbringing which is currently being criticised. They do not provoke the same sense of outrage as some other abusers who inflict very obvious injury on children. (They may, however, contribute to such harm by their failure to protect.) They are struggling with major environmental deficits, of which financial poverty is only one, which make us feel ashamed of the society in which we live. Uncertainty about thresholds interacts again with such feelings and may lead to a kind of passivity on the part of the workers. One of the social workers in research conducted in the 1990s (Allsopp & Stevenson, 1995) expressed his concern about the predicament of the women who were his clients and his anxieties about the role in which he was placed, in which authority (including the courts') had to be exercised to protect the children at times from an alcoholic mother.

> 'I think that women get a rough deal anyway out of society and they have been dumped, they've all been deserted by their men, they've always been used and abused by men all through their lives, their fathers have abused them, their boyfriends/husbands and here we come along, male social workers. We start using and abusing them . . . we're punishing them for what society's done to them.' (Allsopp & Stevenson, 1995, p. 34)

The duty (morally as well as legally) to put the neglected children first never requires us to lose sympathy with the parents; it does, however, require us, on occasion, to act as decisively to protect children as we do in other types of abuse, a fact of which that social worker was well aware.

As if the above were not difficult enough, there is a second strand of particular relevance to social workers at the present time. That is, the loss of confidence in the capacity of the system to provide good enough alternatives to parental care. There is a profound sense of pessimism about present arrangements for 'looking after children'; the extent to which this pessimism is justified cannot be explored here, but it is bound to colour judgements and actions about children neglected in their homes. Again, we are in a vicious circle; the longer children remain at home in unsatisfactory circumstances, the harder it may be for substitute care to be beneficial.

This short chapter sets out the framework which I shall use in seeking to understand the phenomenon of neglect, as it was described in the preface, and in considering purposeful intervention.

The broad outline of the framework is one which is applicable in principle to all work with families where children are 'in need' or need protection. (Indeed it has still wider application.) But the emphasis that is put on the various aspects of family functioning will vary greatly according to the nature of the problems which the families present. As we shall see in the families with which we are here concerned, there are particular difficulties and tensions in balancing and integrating the various factors involved.

The approach chosen here therefore has two strands. First, as Figure 1.1 illustrates, the widely used 'ecological' model enables us to examine a wide range of factors which affect such parents in common with many others. Second, however, it further enables us to focus on particular factors which research or experience suggest are of especial relevance to the predicament of these families. Thus, for example, Chapter 3 examines the impact of social isolation in the lives of these families.

Figure 1.1 is a stylised and simplistic diagram to indicate a systemic approach to the subject; it suggests that just as family members interact with each other, so the family both collectively and individually relates to the world outside. There are a number of dimensions. First, there is the 'nuclear' family, within which individuals interact. Second, there is the wider family. Third, there is the local community, within which there are a number of potential supports; the informal, friends, neighbours, etc.; the semi-formal, such as playgroups for babies or toddlers; and the formal, such as health visitor services or children's centres. Finally, there is wider society which provides the overarching structures of law and governance, including social policies, and which influences families in all kinds of ways, especially through the media. *Families and the individuals within them interact with all these wider systems, both directly, and indirectly through other systems.*

This model emphasises a holistic view of family functioning and implies that change and development occur, for better or for worse, in a number of dimensions. It does less than justice, however, to the complex processes by which individuals and families internalise social and cultural norms and values so that the world outside lives in the minds and feelings of those within the family. Thus, for example, at a

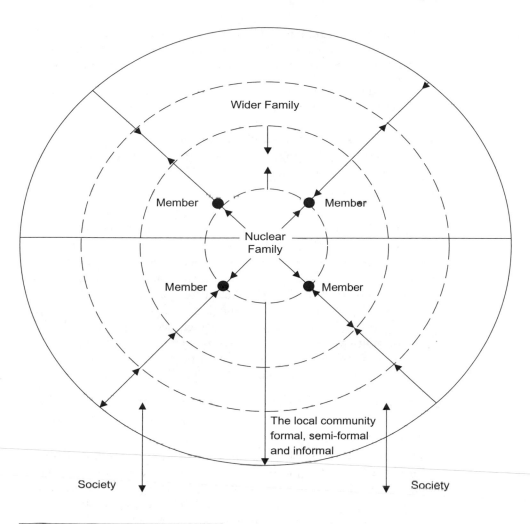

Wider Family

Member

Member

Nuclear
Family

Member

Member

The local community
formal, semi-formal
and informal

Society

Society

Key

→ ← Are examples of
interactions between
individuals and systems

Figure 1.1 Ecological factors in child neglect.

very early age, children absorb social expectations concerning gender, not only from their parents but also from a wide range of other influences from school to television, to which they are subjected.

The model also shows that both the family as a system and the individuals within it are affected collectively and severally by the external forces which impinge on them. For example, one particular child's relationship with an adult outside his/her family or with other children in the locality may be of positive or negative significance in his/her development.

This approach to understanding family functioning has been more and more influential in recent years. The early work of Bronfenbrenner (1979) laid the foundations for a systems model for analysing the social ecology of families (Jack, 2000, p. 702). It can, of course, be utilised in relation to all families, at least in developed societies. However, it is of particular value in considering neglectful families. Gaudin (1993) describes and summarises the literature concerning wide-ranging factors which interact in cases of neglect and concludes that, despite the relative paucity of research on neglect as compared with other kinds of maltreatment, 'it is clear, from existing studies and from the experience of practitioners, that there is no single cause of the inadequate parenting we term child neglect' (p. 11).

This position is now widely accepted and supported by evidence from a range of research explored in later chapters. Garbarino and Collins (1999) convincingly argue that:

'A systems approach helps to clarify the complexity we face in understanding the interplay of biological, psychological, social and cultural forces in neglect. An ecologically grounded systems approach helps us discover connections that might otherwise remain invisible.' (Garbarino & Collins, 1999)

According to Harbin (1980) the first law of ecology is that 'you can never do just one thing' (p. 4). Whilst this 'first law' does not apply to all situations in which families are perceived to need help, it is nearly always true for seriously neglectful families. Jack (2000), arguing the case for an ecological approach to social work with children and families, makes a crucial point which has particular salience for those who work with neglected children.

'The approach . . . is not something which can merely be added to the social workers' toolkit of skills and techniques . . . Rather, it should be thought of as the toolkit itself. It is the cultural environment within which all other policies and practices should be developed.' (Jack, 2000, p. 713)

It cannot, Jack asserts, simply be 'bolted on'.

It may be that today's students and practitioners are more receptive to thinking in ecological terms because of the growing awareness of these subtle and extensive interactions in the worlds of biology and zoology. However, such awareness can lead to a sense of being overwhelmed, of powerlessness, in the face of these complexities. For those who work with neglectful families, it is important to stress that this broad approach in no way diminishes the value of specific theory within the overall framework. For example, knowledge of attachment disorders and their effect on children's behaviour may be crucial to intervention at certain times, whereas, at others, recognition of the impact of financial stress on parental behaviour and interaction may be regarded as the first priority for action. An understanding of systems theory involves recognition that any intervention at a particular aspect of interaction can have positive or negative effects on the whole. The downward 'vicious circle' of a spiral is not the only possibility. There is also the benign circle, brought about by timely and appropriate action on a specific issue.

However, a further point which arises from an acceptance of the ecological model is the necessity of developing effective working together across agencies and professions so that the expertise of all can be pooled. Whilst this has been generally accepted and the focus of government guidance over many years, frequent gross failures have been documented in a range of inquiry reports and research studies. Less well understood has been the relevance of this model to the issue of 'social exclusion', the focus of extensive government effort since 1997 (Jack, 2000; Ghate & Hazel, 2002; Spencer & Baldwin, 2005). Acceptance of an ecological model, within which various other theories can sit quite comfortably, does not absolve us of a responsibility to consider the *weight* which we give to the various factors which contribute to serious child neglect. It is useless to see the problems in isolation, whether they be poverty, immature dysfunctional parenting or environmental stress. We will be left with choices, dependent in part on particular expertise as well as professional or individual preference, as to the focus of the work in certain situations and at certain times.

Although there are dimensions to the concept of social exclusion which are particularly salient to our contemporary society, there are strong resonances with the earlier concentration on 'the cycle of deprivation' in the 1970s (Rutter & Madge, 1976; Fuller & Stevenson, 1983). Whilst the word 'cycle' with its determinist implications, seen by many as suggesting individual pathology, was largely discredited, the issues raised, especially in relation to seriously neglected children, are strongly similar. Although such families are not exclusively to be found in particular geographical areas and neighbourhoods, there is little doubt that the majority will be found in locations, characterised by multiple deprivation at every level and in many ways, in which deficits in environmental, health and educational provision stand out. The conditions of far too many families, as graphically shown by Ghate and Hazel (2002) has been recognised by the government and efforts to combat this social exclusion must be respected; the difficulties in achieving improvements must also be acknowledged. There is, however, a worrying possibility. If there is some success in 'lifting' significant numbers of families out of the grosser aspects of social deprivation, it seems all too likely that the families who are the focus of this book will be further exposed as singularly difficult to help. That could set in train processes of blame and stigmatisation which would simply further oppress and alienate those who, seemingly, we cannot reach. This is why a multi-factorial approach is indispensable.

Conclusion

If we return to Figure 1.1, we can begin to identify many dimensions, explored in later chapters, which are critical to understanding and intervention in these families. These include:

- The differing capacities of particular parents and children.
- The quality of interaction between family members, especially between mothers and infants.
- The relationship between the parents and their own parents which may be highly significant, both positively and negatively.
- The social isolation of such families from the community.
- The family's often highly problematic relationships with the formal sector.
- Their relationships within the local neighbourhood are often highly problematic.
- Their well-being is crucially affected by a range of social policies which affect their material well-being, their health and their education.

Such an approach, however, does not mean that all such factors can be, or need be, given equal emphasis at a particular point in time, or that individual workers can or should pay attention to them all. It does, however, imply the need for a coordinated strategy which, because of the complex problems such families present, will necessarily involve interprofessional and interagency cooperation at a sophisticated level, involving a wider range of workers than heretofore.

This chapter clarifies and summarises the particular problems and dilemmas which arise for practitioners and managers in relation to seriously neglectful families. These are in part definitional; in part arise from doubts about the grounds for specific action; and, more generally, occur because of the complex and anxiety-provoking feelings which are aroused in those who engage with such families.

This chapter has also sought to provide a kind of map to guide us through very confusing terrain.

Neglectful Families:
The General Context

Poverty

Most of this chapter is concerned with social and 'cultural influences'. However, there are many ways in which formal systems in the State and at local government level impinge on all families. The only aspect of this which is discussed here is related to financial and material well-being because it is of critical significance to neglectful families.

Nearly all the families with which this book is concerned are poor, whether that term is used to describe their financial situation or their material quality of life. However, most workers directly involved do not accept that poverty alone creates the difficulties with which they grapple. In the first edition of this book, I commented that social workers had been at the centre of a struggle between competing theories to explain the functioning of families who are offered services, particularly between intra- and interpersonal theories and those which are rooted in a structural analysis of people's problems. In the latter structural analysis, poverty was often seen as of paramount significance and social workers were accused of neglecting its importance.

As was argued in the earlier chapter, there seems to be a growing consensus that the 'either/or' arguments in relation to seriously neglectful families are futile. An ecological model, such as that earlier outlined, places upon us a responsibility to examine the various factors and the interaction between them. If this is taken seriously in the processes of assessment and intervention with particular families, the pervasive effects of poverty in family functioning will be identified and steps taken to ease it. However, this has to be part of what might be termed an 'ecological understanding' which seeks to make connections. Thus, it is not usually helpful for cash or material help to be provided in isolation from other help to chronically 'not coping' families.

This was well illustrated in the report on 'Paul' who died as a result of gross neglect (The Bridge Consultancy, 1995). The Bridge Consultancy noted that:

> 'Considerable amounts of money were provided to the parents to buy furnishings and equipment, which was subsequently sold. We have noted at least three periods when this occurred . . . Considerable general funding, over many years, was provided by Neighbourhood Services, plus several hundreds of pounds raised by health visitors from charitable trusts, which seemed to have little effect on the family's situation.' (The Bridge Consultancy, 1995, p. 152)

Similarly, in the course of the review into Stephanie Fox's death (Lynch & Stevenson, 1990) it became apparent that nearly £1000 had been paid to the family (in small amounts) during the year preceding Stephanie's death. Yet this type of help may not form part of a coordinated plan, may be essentially reactive to family financial crises and rarely seems to improve matters.

Workers exchange many stories of such help disappearing into the chaos and confusion of the household. Yet, once we begin to differentiate between these seriously neglectful families, it will become easier to give such help appropriately, for example a significant offer of material help at a certain point could be of great significance to a depressed mother who is beginning to emerge from the pervasive gloom. It might be of little use at an earlier stage, or to the more chaotic households.

The publication of the *Assessment Framework* (DoH, 2000a) and associated guidance (DoH, 2000b) marked an important step in ensuring that 'family and environmental factors' are placed within the 'three interrelated systems or domains' (DoH, 2000a, p. 17), the detailed implications of which will be explored in later chapters. (See Figure 2.1.) Within the sub-headings of the main guidance in the bottom line of the triangle, there is a reference to 'income' but the subsequent comment on such matters (DoH, 2000a) is very thin, even taking into account that the documents are intended for use in a far wider context than the very small group of neglected families who are our focus (DoH, 2000b, p. 99, paras 3.120–122). In the 'Family Pack of Questionnaires and Scales' (DoH, 2000a), the omission of material designed to assess the impact of poverty is striking. For example, in the 'Parenting

Figure 2.1   The Assessment Framework. Department of Health (2000) *Framework for the Assessment of Children in Need and their Families.* Stationery Office, London.

Daily Hassle Scale' (p. 20 H), there is no item to ascertain the difficulties for parents when children argue or complain about their 'need' for various items. Nor is there anything in the 'adolescent well-being' scale (p. 32) to suggest that this issue might be problematic. In the 'Recent Life Events' (p. 36), three out of twenty-one items are connected with poverty, two on employment and one on 'major' financial difficulties, such as debt or difficulty paying bills. Overall, however, the impression given is of much greater emphasis on other aspects of family functioning.

This is surprising, given the growing awareness of the extent of child poverty in the UK. The government has committed itself to the 'abolition' of child poverty by 2020 and, although the target may not be met, there is no doubt of the determined efforts which have been made to improve the position. The scale of the task is indicated by the bald figures which show that the number of children in households on below half average incomes grew from one in ten in 1968 to just under one in three between 1968 and 1995–96. Since 1997, efforts to reduce inequality have been masked by rising incomes at the top of the income scale. Despite this, the latest figures show that in 2003–04, one in five and one in six (depending on housing costs) of children in Great Britain lived in households 60% below average/median income (Horton, 2005). It is shameful that, in a league table of Child Poverty in Rich Countries (Unicef, 2000), the United Kingdom is placed nineteenth out of twenty five, with 15.4% of children living in 'relative poverty', defined as households with income below 50% of the national average. (The lowest, Denmark, was 2.4%.)

There are various implications of this discussion for seriously neglectful families. It is clear that they are amongst the most vulnerable in terms of the interaction of their poverty with the other factors associated with their problems. The children at greatest risk of poverty include those in lone parent households, in workless households and in large families and where the mother is under 25 (Department for Work and Pensions, 2003). These are all factors frequently associated with the families we are considering.

Of particular importance is the effect of 'financial stressors' admirably described by Ghate and Hazel (2002). Their study, *Parenting in Poor Environments*, is of the various factors associated with parenting under stress. Their large sample was chosen from geographical areas in which there were high levels of social and material disadvantage. They write: 'Financial strains loomed large in this sample. Indeed, it is difficult to overrate the importance of financial difficulties as a source of stress in the daily lives of families in poor environments' (p. 65). To workers in this field, it will not come as a surprise that significant numbers of parents (in a sample of 1754) could not afford even day trips once a year, heating whenever it was needed, or basic toys or sports gear for children. The authors go further, however, in discussing 'the way in which the constant efforts of managing money and making ends meet creates a sense of stress and strain for parents that permeates family life' (pp. 67–8). They found that significant proportions of their sample were worried about money and that there was a strong inverse association between household income levels and parental 'malaise' score. Apart from the obvious complaint of 'not enough money', one in five referred to unexpected or unusual expenses, to chronic long-term debts (apart from a mortgage) of two or more years standing; a similar number report getting behind with repayments, or being hassled by credit company lenders or other lenders. 'In total, out of those who identified they were not managing well financially, nearly one third cited credit and debit repayments as part of the problem' (p. 69). Ghate and Hazel did not find 'fecklessness', or mismanagement, were often part of the problem, although it is likely that in those families we are considering, 'mismanagement' will be seen to be part of the overall problem. However, this should not blind workers to the fact that the parents may be faced with insoluble difficulties. It is essential that workers involved (and it will usually be the social worker) take responsibility for plumbing the depths of the financial problems which beset particular parents. This will not be simple; there will often be an understandable reluctance to admit these, especially where unscrupulous moneylenders feature in their lives. It may be necessary to enlist those with financial expertise to sort out what can be done.

Whilst the present government has put in place a range of measures to address child poverty, of which Child Tax Credits are an important example, it remains of concern and is of particular relevance to 'our' families, that there is an acceptance in official policy that families in poverty, as defined by the State, can routinely pay back to, or via, the State a substantial amount of their basic income in respect of arrears for essential household services or goods. Deduction at source may be of two kinds. First, they may be made for arrears in payments of housing costs, gas, electricity, water, fines, social fund loans and overpayment of income support. No more than three deductions can be made (in the above order of priority) and there are tight limits to the amounts which can be deducted. Second, deductions for current payments for necessities such as electricity and gas may be made. Up to 25% of the total benefit can be taken at source without the claimants' consent.

The Department of Work and Pensions would prefer not to operate a quasi-banking service, but others argue that such arrangements are in fact in the claimants' interest – to avoid disconnections and the installation of pre-payment meters which are more expensive. Whatever the advantages of present arrangements, these procedures muffle the protests and public criticisms which would be heard if the families had to do without basic goods and services. But if some families, many of whom will have other debts as well, can have up to 25% of their benefit deducted at source, the longer-term effects of living on an income well below basic subsistence must be serious, especially in relation to nutrition and health. Although the policy of compulsory deductions may on occasion avoid dire consequences, government policy itself has added to the poverty of some families. As Becker (1997) points out, the introduction of social fund loans in the 1980s was 'the first time in post-war British social security policy that the poorest claimants have been expected to repay money given to them to meet their exceptional needs' (p. 66). He described as 'particularly repugnant' the policy of refusing some loans on the grounds that claimants would be unable to pay them back (Becker, 2003). Some have argued that the existence of interest-free social fund loans provides a better alternative than having to resort to the commercial sector or loan shark. Whilst this may be so, it is indefensible that the State can deduct up to a quarter of a family's benefit and, in my view, it is morally dubious that any sum should be deducted from benefits set at subsistence level.

The social fund is discretionary and is meant to help people on a low income to meet one-off expenses on necessities and in emergencies through community care grants, budgeting loans, and crisis loans. A recent thorough study, initiated by the Joseph Rowntree Foundation, (Beckhelling *et al.*, 2006) confirmed the impression given by many workers in the field that it makes little impact on the position of poor families. 'The overwhelming experience of participants was [that the fund did not help them] to meet their needs, as often applications were refused or only a partial award was granted' (Beckhelling *et al.*, 2006, pp. 94–95). The authors point out that the fund does not reduce poverty when awards are received as loans, which are repaid through deductions from benefits. They found that in February 2005, the average weekly deduction from Income Support was £11.24.

It can be assumed that the families we are considering will benefit little from the social fund. The authors point out that benefit recipients experienced social exclusion in two main ways: by being unable to participate in everyday activities and by being unable to meet the additional educational costs of school uniform, equipment, school trips and children's clothing. Amongst their proposals for discretionary grants are: regular, though modest, start of school grants and essential items grants (for particular circumstances, such as starting a new home or the break-up of a household). They also discuss more constructive ways in which loans might be given for specific circumstances.

However, even if changes are effected, the role of the social fund is relatively minor in relation to the overall poverty in which so many of 'our' families find themselves (which is not, of course, to disparage the constructive proposals outlined above). Clearly, the issue is inseparable from policies to help parents into employment whenever possible. Since coming into power in 1997, the government has put in place a range of policies to facilitate return to employment and reduce 'benefit dependency'. Yet what we know of the characteristics of neglectful parents suggests that they will need very considerable social and psychological help before they are even at the starting block. It seems unlikely that staff employed at government agencies, particularly Job Centre Plus, will be able to offer adequate help to the parents whom we are considering, without specialist training and advice. Nor is it clear who will be available to offer this.

Poverty on the scale experienced by most 'neglectful families' creates unremitting strain and disadvantage. One hopes, and is entitled to assume, that this dimension is well appreciated by those who work with such families. The challenge is to incorporate that dimension of understanding as part of an active plan for support and intervention; hitherto, action in poverty has too often been reactive, for example, the 'Friday afternoon, no giro' phenomenon, without a sense of continuity and purpose.

However, it is unfair to place the responsibility for this on field workers. For children's services in social service departments, organisational ambivalence about its discretionary powers has given them little training or policy guidance about their constructive use. For both social workers and health visitors (and perhaps other professionals) the complex causes and effects of poverty, debt and mismanagement in neglectful families have been given insufficient emphasis in training and staff development so that there is sometimes a naive reliance on material help to alleviate much more deep-seated difficulties.

The tasks for those involved at field level are therefore:

- To know the details of this family's financial position, including debt and deductions from benefit and to ensure full entitlement is secured.
- To seek to understand and to feel the impact of poverty on individual members of this family – which deficits are felt most keenly by children and adults.
- To consider the particular difficulties in managing which this family experiences.
- In the light of the above, to identify and integrate financial advice or assistance into a protection plan.

However, the responsibility for the alleviation of poverty obviously goes beyond the workers at field level. Leaving aside wider questions of the adequacy of benefit levels, the problems of deductions of social fund grants and loans, and (closely connected) of the local authority's exercise of its discretionary powers all need to be considered urgently. They have a particular relevance to the families with whom we are concerned.

As Figure 1.1 indicated, there is a constant dynamic interplay between, on the one hand, the family and the individuals which comprise it and, on the other, the various systems and groups of people outside it. Most of this chapter seeks to understand those families in which children are neglected, with reference to informal systems – the wider family, the neighbourhood and cultural influences. There is a substantial research literature, much of it from the USA, which demonstrates that families in which children are seriously neglected are, in comparison with other families, very socially isolated (Polansky *et al.*, 1985a; b). Polansky argues that this social isolation is found in families of abused children generally. However, this is challenged by Seagull (1987), who claims that the research evidence for this is much stronger in the case of neglect than in other kinds of abuse. She also points to the associated finding that many neglectful families bring this isolation upon themselves. Gaudin (1993), summarising the findings for the US Department of Health and Human Services, concludes: 'Neglectful parents typically lack strong informal helpful resources' (p. 18). This is the observation of many practitioners in this country and is confirmed by such research in the UK as that of Creighton (1986). She examined the information on children registered for neglect in the two previous years and found that social isolation was the second highest of 37 factors which workers were asked to rank in order of their severity of effect.

Before further discussing the evidence of social isolation, however, we need to remind ourselves that the phrase 'social isolation' carries within it a value judgement. Isolation is deemed to be undesirable and suggests that there is a deficit which must be made good. Whilst this will be a reasonable goal in many aspects and domains of the lives of parents and children, when it is applied indiscriminately it may distract attention from the negative or damaging effects of some kinds of interaction.

Wider family and community support

The British study by Ghate and Hazel (2002), referred to earlier in this chapter, throws light on the complicated factors at work in relation to the concepts of social isolation and social exclusion. Although their study dealt with a much larger group of families than those we are here considering, it is safe to say that most of 'our' families will fall within that broader group. Ghate and Hazel examined informal support, its extent and its type. They do not in general differentiate between wider family and friends. However, their findings are highly relevant to neglectful families. They found that, even in the socially deprived neighbourhoods which were the focus of the study, most parents professed themselves well supported in terms of numbers of supporters and frequency of contact. However, those who reported more restricted networks than others included some of those who had the highest levels of problems.

They point out that, nonetheless, and 'arguably more important', there were notable limits in terms of actual, enacted informal support (p. 125). In reality, when asked to describe precisely *what* support they received, parents were much less clear about their ability to enlist support when they needed it. The authors point out that this may reflect, in part, parents' own attitudes or willingness to accept help. The characteristics which Ghate and Hazel identify in those less well supported accord with the experience of practitioners in working with neglectful families. They conclude:

> 'The final results indicated that the odds of not coping well in poor environments were particularly increased for parents if they had greater numbers of dependent children, had a difficult child, exhibited a tendency to depression . . . reported high levels of personal and family difficulties . . . or were parenting alone . . . For each additional problem experienced by parents, the chances of not coping were almost doubled . . . It gives us a vivid indication of how problems can pile up to reduce parents' sense of being able to manage their lives.' (Ghate & Hazel, 2002, p. 196)

Whether one is examining the nuclear or the wider family, an analysis of power and influence is inevitable. In the families we are here considering, it is too easy to move from the observation that they are often isolated in certain ways from their relatives to the assumption that it would be good to lessen the isolation. But that is naive, unless we take into account that in the course of seeking to improve the quality of these interactions we may bring to the surface negative as well as positive emotions or may seem to reinforce power in certain members of the family or other groups through legitimising their intervention. There is a particular danger, a false logic, in moving from the finding that neglectful families are 'in deficit' socially to an assumption that more 'input' from existing sources is needed to make good the deficit. As Gaudin (1993) points out: 'The social networks of neglectful mothers appear to be dominated by relatives who are critical rather than supportive. Interactions with relatives may be frequent but not very helpful' (p. 18). As Seagull (1987) tersely puts it: 'Considering the very negative rearing of the majority of abusive parents, staying away from their parents could be indicative of good judgement' (p. 49).

It is surprising how little attempt there has been in the study of families and children to disentangle the complex issues surrounding the notion of 'support' by a network of relatives from other kinds of social support. There has been more work in the field of adult community care, some of which (for example Finch (1989) who explores 'obligations' of family members to each other) would repay application to other areas of family life. The so-called 'nuclear' families which are the focus of our concern are often lone mothers with unstable partnerships. I know of no systematic study in this country concerning the quality of relationships between such mothers and their relatives.

In the USA, Coohey (1995) examined the significance of mutual aid between neglectful mothers and their mothers. She comments that 'despite the burgeoning literature, no study in the child maltreatment area has focused on the exchange relations between abusive mothers and their mothers' (p. 886). In a carefully constructed, multicultural study she reached the following interesting conclusions, from the accounts of the neglectful mothers themselves: 'Mothers of neglectful mothers when compared with others, are either less willing or less able to give emotional support to their neglectful daughters and neglectful daughters are less interested in receiving emotional support' (p. 893).

Coohey acknowledges that from these findings we cannot conclude the extent to which the present reflects past patterns: whether the older woman's inability to give to her daughter as a child is carried through to adult life. However, it seems probable. In general, neglectful daughters said they received 'significantly less emotional and instrumental support from their mothers' (p. 893). (There was, however, a very significant unexplained exception of potential importance: very little difference between the sample and control group on help with baby-sitting.) The general findings should not be viewed too pessimistically. The amount of help and mutual support offered in these exchanges was still significant, even if less than in the control group. For example, 41% of these 'neglectful' mothers described their mothers as 'really listening/providing companionship'; 49% gave money or loans.

The above describes only one, small-scale study from another country, of one dimension, adult mother–daughter relationships which affect the well-being of families. It is cited here to bring to the fore the need for sensitivity to, and detailed appreciation of, the significance of such family relationships. Neither of these general propositions, that support of the wider family is valuable and the specific observation that abusive and neglectful parents frequently lack such support, is controversial amongst professionals. It will be 'nodded through' at conferences. Yet there seems to be a disjunction between this acceptance and a real understanding of its particular significance. Indeed, 'family, friends and neighbours' are often lumped together in discussion. Yet, when neglectful families are isolated from their wider network of relatives, the implications are particularly grave. They are cut off from a source of support and help which is of immense significance to most families (McGlone *et al.*, 1996). This help may be 'instrumental' or 'affective' (Polansky, 1985b). In well-functioning families these are often inseparable and interact to positive effect. The type of instrumental help which is commonest is of two kinds. There are small-scale financial transactions; loans and gifts, or gifts in kind, may offer a day-by-day lifeline to those in poverty. Indeed, they may reduce dependence on debt from exploitative lenders. Second, sharing in the care of children in diverse ways relieves stress and opens up employment opportunities. Both these forms of support are affected by the position and age of the older generation. The younger the mothers, the more likely it is that the older generation will still be caught up in their own child rearing and employment and have less to offer to their adult children and grandchildren.

'Affective' help is less tangible but profoundly important; the offering of advice and sympathy, the taken-for-granted currency of everyday interaction, may have particularly positive effects when offered within close emotional relationships. These relationships are not all mediated via the adults to the children; not infrequently, the children, individually, relate to particular relatives who may offer them a supplement to, or different dimension from, life at home. The ordinary price that is paid for such support is exposure to a certain amount of tension, conflict, hurt and anger. But, as Seagull (1987) suggests, that price may be too high for some neglectful parents who have learned not to get too psychologically close to others, for fear of being emotionally hurt (p. 48).

In the *Framework for the Assessment of Children and their Families* (DoH, 2000a), the bottom line of the triangle, 'Family and Environmental Factors', includes the 'wider family' in this process (see Figure 2.1). The Practice Guidance (DfES, 2006) alludes to the issue at various points in the document: in the general section, (paras 36 and 38); in the section on black children (paras 37–69, 2.152–2.155); and on disabled children (paras 70–103, 108, 110). It is unfortunate that there is no specific examination of the matter in relation to children who are neither black nor disabled, in particular those who have been identified as the most at risk, by being placed on the register. The general comment at 1.38 notes that: 'The role of the wider family can be a significant source of support. Conversely, extended families may not always be supportive.' They refer to Thoburn *et al.* (2000). However, in the context of the assessment framework, there is little to guide practitioners in their exploration of the complexities of the relationships which are so critical to the understanding of a nuclear family's current problems when there is serious neglect. It is at this point, when the past meets the present, that parenting of the children is crucially affected by earlier internalised images of their own parents and by the current attitudes of the wider family. Also important in this past–present continuum are the relationships with siblings, especially between sisters, which in well-functioning families are often a source of much support.

Farmer and Owen (1995) made perceptive comments which take us further in understanding the significance of this subject. They point out that, in investigating child abuse and neglect, workers often did not clarify relationships with the wider family even in 'stocktaking' occasions such as the case conference: 'The lack of family support or social isolation was not always known. Even when it had been discussed, *it was often treated as a matter for counselling*' (p. 285).

This, of course, is the nub of the matter. As we have shown, the extent and nature of wider family supports, their strengths and deficiencies, are important in the here and now, in making assessments and purposeful plans for the present situation. It is not simply a 'matter for counselling'. It is also important in understanding more of what Farmer and Owen describe as the 'aetiology' of the abuse or neglect, or 'the germ of an explanatory theory'. This explanatory theory is not simply of historical interest (how did these parents come to be as they are?), but also of immediate relevance to the present family situation. As we shall discuss later, it is imperative to search for the meaning of parental 'omissions' – what is it that they cannot do for their children and why? How far is this related to the care which they in turn were not given? What, therefore, should professionals be trying to achieve in relation to these wider family relationships? Farmer and Owen point out that 'information was presented in a disconnected way or linked simply to the diagnosis or risk'. Therefore, its 'implication for planning often went unrecognised' (pp. 136–7).

That these deficiencies in the approach to work with families have been acknowledged in the influential research discussed above gives cause for some optimism, as did the receptive professional audience for the notion of 'family group conferences', which originated in New Zealand. These developments were described at length by Marsh and Crow (1997). The process itself of mobilising relatives to discuss and plan for children in difficulty will not be discussed here. Rather, it is used as an illustration of the underlying importance of the general approach to the involvement of family members. As Marsh and Crow point out, the evidence of the importance of the family network for nearly all families is powerful and 'pivotal in child welfare'. Furthermore, 'diversity is the hallmark of the modern family, with values, employment patterns, culture, race and many other factors interacting and resulting in a unique blend for each family' (p. 28). To start with, as they succinctly put it: 'to work with the family, we have to ask the family who the family is' (p. 30). They view the wider family as a 'psychosocial entity' in which different members, over time, exert more or less influence. They discuss the meaning and impact which the wider family group has on its subsystem, in particular, the part it plays in the development of a child's identity.

Nearly a decade has passed since the Marsh and Crow publications, at which time there was probably more enthusiasm for the idea of family group conferences amongst some (probably not many) practitioners and social work leaders than there is now. The Family Rights Group were influential in this. Brown (2003) 'examined the extent to which family group conferences have developed and become embedded in current social work practice' (p. 331). She notes that the Department of Health took a neutral position until the end of the 1990s (DoH, 1999) when they described these conference processes as 'a positive option for planning services' (p. 78). However, they were insistent that such conferences could not replace the long-established child protection conference. It is hard to see how anyone would have seen them as an alternative, given the legal and procedural framework in place for protection from significant harm. However, some have argued that the essence of the model posed challenges to professional power value systems and organisational expectations. Questions were raised as to whether managers and practitioners were able to accept a 'fundamental shift in power towards families' (Brown, 2003, p. 332). Brown, reporting on the results of national UK surveys in 1999 and 2001, found that there was considerable variation in the extent to which particular cases were referred for this purpose and no firm evidence as to their outcomes.

Family group conferences can be utilised in several different contexts, for example child welfare, education, youth justice and domestic violence. More recently, as Brown (2003) points out, they have been identified as potentially useful in cases of potential adoption (Cabinet Office, 2000, p. 63). Seriously neglectful families will often present problems related to those issues listed above and this offers the possibility of constructive intervention which involves the wider family. However, a decision to convene such a conference must rest on an assessment which examines the nature of these existing relationships and makes a judgement as to the extent to which those concerned are capable and willing to put the interests of the neglected children at the top of the agenda of family dynamics. It should not be assumed that resistance to using this method arises only from professional reluctance to cede power to the family or, more prosaically, resource constraints, although both of these may come into play. Assessment in such cases will include an appraisal of the extent to which a particular family shows obvious similarities or differences in problematic parenting patterns. This will obviously have a bearing on the judgement as to whether they are likely and/or suitable to help.

There is one way, however, in which this trend may be seen to be part of a more substantial development and thus likely to have a more permanent impact on child welfare work. The movement towards greater inclusion and involvement of family members in the lives of particular families is associated with earlier work towards 'partnership' with parents, which has been extensively researched and discussed in research in the 1990s. (See, for example, Thoburn *et al.*, 1995.) It is part of an ethos in which power should be more effectively and sincerely shared by professionals with those we describe as 'informal carers', who usually play the most critical part in the lives of the children upon whom our concern is focused. However, as with the concepts of 'partnership with parents', there has to be a determined effort neither to idealise nor to minimise the capacity of relatives to meet the deficits for children so often found in neglectful families. The way to avoid either extreme has to be by systematic exploration of these unique interactions. Whether or not the specific technique of the family group conference is used, the key task is to make some sense of the relationships between family members to find some coherent patterns between family needs and deficits, to ask what has been on offer in the past and what might be offered in the future. The worker's image of the family needs to be expanded, so that the potential and limitations of the wider family network in relation to the needs of the nuclear family are better understood.

Social exclusion

During the decade since the first edition of this book, the term 'social exclusion' has been brought into professional language by the government. It describes well the position of many of the families with whom the book is concerned, but it may have particularly intense connotations. For many of them, material and financial disadvantage is not the only stigmatising factor. Indeed, they may have this in common with others in the same geographical area, even though it marks them out from the wider community. Some of these families have been described, and further stigmatised, by television programmes about 'the neighbours from hell'. Their behaviour is shown to have alienated them from their immediate neighbourhood. They become pariahs and, inevitably, show strong hostility to those who are rejecting them. It is a very powerful dynamic which is exceedingly difficult to alter.

Ethnic and cultural factors

There are serious difficulties in relating the topic of this book, neglect, to ethnic and cultural factors in ways which will be helpful to practitioners. Some problems arise from the lack of research and knowledge in the UK in this area. There are three dimensions to this: first, we need much more detailed information about the child rearing practices of particular groups. These are subtle processes which cannot be viewed through a telescope. Second, we need to know what difficulties or changes of behaviour arise from living as a minority group within a majority culture. Third, the above has to be applied to the problem of neglect. However, as we shall see, this relative dearth of knowledge is itself significant because of the anxiety and sensitivity surrounding the investigation of culture. Nonetheless, in my view, the time is overdue for an attempt to discuss these extremely important issues.

The term 'culture' is used here to mean patterns of shared experience and behaviour through which personal identity and social structures are developed. Culture is thus a concept which extends beyond race and ethnicity and, in our context, has particular salience in terms of social class as well as ethnic difference. However, we do well also to remind ourselves that ethnicity does not only mean 'non-white'. Rather, it refers to the distinctive identity of particular groups, derived in part from racial, religious and cultural affiliations. It is important, also, to recognise that racial, ethnic and even class origins are not, of themselves, sufficient to explain variations in child rearing. Culture is located within prevailing norms and values in which there are contradictions and tensions and in which present norms and values may clash with those passed on from families of origin. This observation is of particular importance in some work with ethnic minorities where, for example, there is sharp tension between parents and teenage girls, although care must be taken not to exaggerate the racial significance of behaviour common to many families of all ethnic groups who have adolescent children.

References to child maltreatment occur throughout history and across cultures. However, since the 1960s, influenced by the focus on the subject in the USA, there has been a burgeoning literature in this area. It has demonstrated wide variations in definition, often bound up with the prevailing economic and social conditions of the time, as well as underlying value systems (Korbin, 1991). There is now general understanding that child abuse is a socially constructed concept and hence susceptible to different interpretation in time and place. Korbin argues that this 'presents a dilemma . . . Failure to allow for a cultural perspective promotes an ethnocentric position in which one's own cultural beliefs and practices are presumed to be preferable and superior to all others.' Yet, 'a stance of extreme cultural relativism in which all judgements of humane treatment of children are suspended in the name of cultural rights, may be used to justify a lesser standard of care for some children' (p. 68). Maitra (1995) argues that culture must be examined, but as part of:

'An examination of the interactive effects of racism, minority status and socio-economic disadvantage with each group's cultural systems. A focus on racial discrimination alone runs the risk of conferring the minority person within two stereotypes – of victim, or its mirror image, the rigidly idealised "black" identity.' (Maitra, 1995, p. 156)

Korbin and Spilsbury (1999) address these issues in relation to child neglect. They stress the importance of 'cultural competence' when social workers attempt to intervene in families whose ethnic and cultural backgrounds differ from the host culture:

'Cultural competence practice puts children's well-being and protection first but understands well-being and protection within the cultural context. Cultural competence incorporates culture in definitions of child neglect to identify cases without cultural bias. Cultural competence addresses the need for a culturally informed perspective on the aetiology of child neglect to better inform culturally appropriate prevention and intervention. Cultural competence helps sort out which aspects of a family's difficulties are "cultural", which are "neglectful", and which are a combination of factors'. (Korbin & Spilsbury, 1999, p. 70)

Their diagram, shown in Figure 2.2, is helpful in focusing the attention of workers on the key issues in such cases.

As Korbin and Spilsbury (1999) point out 'identification of neglect is firmly rooted in cultural and societal standards within which the acceptability of parental behaviour and the severity of child outcomes are judged' (p. 76). The most basic need is for survival itself and they suggest that in that primary goal there is little evidence of significant cultural difference. Social workers should not expect to find major variations in practices designed to keep babies and young children safe in relation to food, hygiene and supervision. Beyond that, however, there are cultural habits and traditions reflecting different values or different levels of awareness of children's needs. Thus, for example, the extent to which education is prized varies; this may raise questions as to whether children's educational needs are being 'neglected'. (This is an interesting example, since it appears that, in the UK, white indigenous families may value education less than some black and Asian families.) Or, in the sphere of health, it may be that the proven importance of certain preventative measures, such as inoculation and vaccination, are simply not understood by recent arrivals to the UK.

In Figure 2.2, box 4c reminds us that some manifestation of neglect reflects a lack of adjustment to the realities of the society in which the family is now living. This is particularly so in cases of children 'left alone', as Thoburn et al., point out (2000). A further issue, in box 4d,

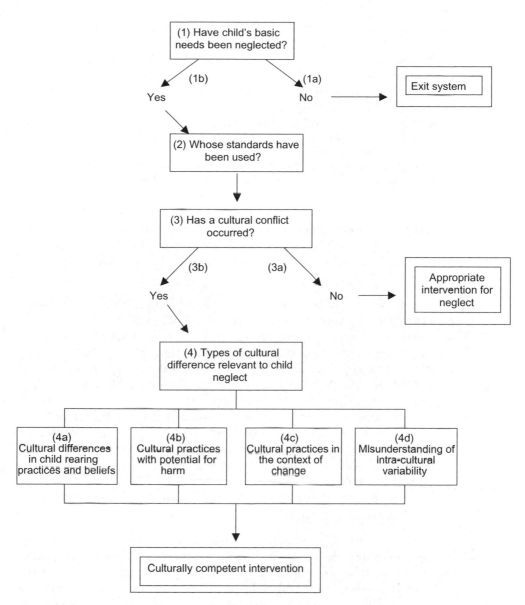

Figure 2.2 Cultural competence in child neglect intervention. (Korbin & Spilsbury, in Dubowitz, 1999).

concerns the 'misunderstanding of intra-cultural variability' (p. 80). This problem has been identified in the UK in a range of serious case reviews concerning maltreatment generally. One of the earliest examples was in the case of Tyra Henry (London Borough of Lambeth, 1987) when the inquiry identified exaggerated expectations of the role of the Afro-Caribbean grandparent. More recently, uncertainty and confusion about cultural values was illustrated in the Victoria Climbié case (Laming, 2000, pp. 345–347), especially in relation to religious beliefs.

The now extensive British literature in child abuse and neglect generally, has not much advanced our understanding of cultural factors within the UK in relation to the problem of neglect, or indeed, of other forms of abuse. Many social workers have thought it preferable to draw attention to the racism which causes suffering to children and families and to expose racist assumptions by professionals rather than to dwell on variations and subtleties of child rearing practices (Dutt & Phillips, 1996).

This is reinforced by the same authors in the *Framework for the Assessment* (DoH Practice Guidance, 2000b, pp. 37–70) which emphasises the dangers of inappropriate or stereotyped views of black children, their families and patterns of child rearing. They rightly point out how much all 'good enough' parents have in common. Yet failure to recognise the significance of culture is in the end a kind of racism. It can result in a kind of professional immobilisation, in which difference may be ignored, or wrongly attributed to cultural difference, rather than to the problems of certain individuals. Underlying this, there is confusion concerning the implications of 'cultural relativism', an inability to sort out what differences in child rearing practices can be acceptable in the context of contemporary society and what cannot be accepted. Channer and Parton (1990) refer to 'reconstructed racism which leads to a failure to act at all' (p. 112).

This is a difficult and delicate matter, but one has only to look at the realities of the dilemmas which child welfare practitioners face in day-to-day work to see that it has to be faced. Some agonising problems centre on issues, such as female genital circumcision, that are outside the scope of this book. But to focus only on such extreme matters distorts the debate. The only honest way to work is to approach families of different origins respectfully, in the expectation that there are likely to be variations in child rearing, and with the curiosity to find out about those which are relevant to the circumstances of the case. This does not absolve the worker from making a judgement, in certain matters, as to whether the care offered is 'good enough' by the standards and knowledge of our time. This is the best we can do. It should ensure that we do not fall into either extreme: of cultural dogmatism that 'ours is the best way', or cultural relativism that 'anything goes'.

A measure of curiosity (some would call it 'nosiness') provided it is focused, is a prerequisite for good professional practice. There has been a puzzling lack of curiosity about this most interesting and important dimension of work with families and children. It is probably best explained in terms of anxiety and fear either of being racist or of being perceived as such. Channer and Parton (1990) argue that 'culturally relative practice must be abandoned since it leads to simplistic, polarised and stereotypical views of clients and their situations and does nothing to challenge workers' own norms and values' (p. 117).

When we come to neglect, there has been virtually no exploration of the application of the concept, its definitions and examples, to different ethnic and cultural groups in the UK. There is no evidence (and one would not expect there to be) that serious neglect, as the term is generally used in this country, is more common amongst one group than another.

Although fascinating, it is probably misleading to place much emphasis on unfamiliar practice from far-off countries. However, some illustrations are of value in raising our sensitivity to the differences in child rearing which might have to be taken into account within the British context. Rashid (1996), for example, examines culture in relation to the theory of attachment. He argues that 'attachment, like bereavement, is shaped or patterned by the culture in which it takes place' (p. 61). He points out that child care professionals might 'attempt to evaluate the strength and nature of the attachment relationship . . . by using culturally, specific notions like direct eye contact' (p. 61). He gives examples of cultures in which gaze is associated with disrespect and discouraged by mothers. In the Gusii (Kenya), it is suggested that child rearing practices are designed to lower competitiveness in mothers and children. This may lead children to appear under stimulated and more passive.

Thus, one of the accepted indicators of neglect (lack of stimulation) is another possible area of difficulty; how much stimulation, of what kind and at what ages is it usually given in the minority groups represented in this country? These questions would merit further study. Dutt and Phillips draw attention to this issue in the assessment practice guidance (DoH, 2000b, p. 60).

Owusa-Bempah and Howitt (1998) also explore theories of attachment in relation to culture. They argue, convincingly, that this body of theory may not adequately address the power of 'socio-genealogical connections', that is the extent to which they root their sense of identity in their natural parents' background even when they do not live with them. Although this does not bear directly on our topic, it reminds us that no body of theory, even one as significant as attachment, can be divorced from its cultural context. The complexities of this issue have been well discussed by O'Hagan (1999), who argues that there has been a failure by social workers to grasp the significance of the concept of culture: 'racism has often been regarded as a more significant issue than culture; the cultural heritage of clients and their families has been perceived as oppressive and culture has been misinterpreted to explain and to tolerate unacceptable behaviour' (p. 269).

More obviously bound to culture and experience are various practices involving health. Whilst there is the same goal, there may be deeply held differences of the means to that end. Korbin (1991) gives an example of Turkish mothers' belief that a child of 18 months must be kept very warm indeed by Western standards (p. 69). A study by Hackett and Hackett (1994) is particularly valuable because it investigated child rearing practices in relation to Gujarati and white British children brought up in the UK. It reminds us of differences of emphasis in upbringing which can reasonably be seen as differing routes to the same goal, that of rearing healthy, well-socialised children. It is interesting that, although closely linked, the differences relate more to other issues of abuse (physical and emotional) than to neglect. For example, British parents believed that smacking was more necessary than Gujarati parents but, in fact, there were few differences between them in reported frequency. Gujarati parents were much less likely to tolerate 'mess' (water, paint, etc.) than British parents, were more punitive about toilet training and bed-wetting, but much more relaxed about bedtimes and sleeping arrangements. Most important, the emotional 'Gujarati preference methods of discipline' (p. 198) (withdrawing love, bringing in an authority figure, etc.) were clear; British parents tended to disapprove of these methods. The Gujarati children were found to be better adjusted, despite the fact that some of their child rearing practices were, by conventional Western standards, less acceptable. Even that finding, however, reminds us that 'adjustment' is itself a culturally contested concept. What is a good child? None of the examples of difference chosen by the authors brought issues of neglect, that is omission of care, to the fore. Rather, they challenged some of the cultural assumptions about 'best ways' of disciplining and bringing up children. However, the cultural differences are within relatively narrow parameters of 'ordinary' upbringing – a far cry from seriously neglectful families.

The above examples are intended to shed light on the fascinating and diverse patterns of child rearing which one is sure to find when cultural norms are explored. Such explorations challenge us at a deep level: in terms of our preconceptions, of our ability to learn from others and our ability to sort out whether what we observe is just different, or worryingly different. If it is the latter, is it worrying because we believe there is an important clash of cultures, or is it because the situation is unacceptable to both cultures? It is thus both emotionally and intellectually demanding and requires a professional person to be as well informed as possible. The present deficiencies in knowledge and research on the subject of 'culture and neglect' make it all the more important to reach into the cultural groups with whom we are working, to utilise fully the knowledge which reposes within those communities. This will help workers to weigh up the significance of what they see, which is especially important when there are a number of possible indicators of neglect under consideration. It is about a holistic picture, in which (with some exceptions) a particular child rearing practice is not in itself a determinant of neglect. It is self-evident that professionals of the same cultural groups are invaluable. But their absence does not excuse lack of curiosity on the part of the others; nor should particular individuals representing particular ethnic groups have to bear too heavy a burden of 'understanding'. Furthermore, the availability of such individuals is of greatest value in raising awareness of and respect for cultural values amongst their colleagues, not to 'ghettoise' services to ethnic minorities (Owusa-Bempah, 1998).

There is a further dimension of this issue to which Korbin (1991) draws attention: that is, the possibility that there are particular categories of children who may be more susceptible to maltreatment, including abuse, than others. This is a highly sensitive matter and one should note that Korbin's analysis relates to cross-cultural differences between countries or continents and does not necessarily take into account the effects of prevailing values on minorities in this country. Part of Korbin's analysis relates to the care of children who may be less valued than others, by reason of their family status (e.g. stepchildren), gender or disability. It is commonly known, for example, that in some countries boys receive preferential treatment, including basic care in infancy. (This preference was also deeply imbedded in British culture in terms, for example, of education and inheritance rights.) Attitudes to children with learning or physical disabilities may be of shame and rejection; this may be difficult to observe since, in some cultures, children may be hidden from view (literally or symbolically). But if they are rejected then neglect may be more serious and cannot be tolerated within our society. Thus, when children are culturally devalued, serious moral issues are posed for the workers. For the rest, Korbin points out that across all cultures particular children in a family may be scapegoated. The reasons given may differ but they are often associated with circumstances of birth.

In addition to raised awareness of cultural variations in child rearing itself, there are important matters concerning the impact on families of the investigative and interventive processes which arise in cases of abuse and neglect. Owusa-Bempah (1998), in an interesting study, has explored the application of principles of confidentiality in social work across cultures, using African culture as an example. He points out that in British society confidentiality assumes an 'individual–community dichotomy', whereas in African cultures the individual derives his or her sense of identity from belonging to a family, group or community (p. 1). However, this may mean that the notion of confidentiality is significant to the family group as a whole and does not necessarily imply a willingness to share information with 'outsiders' such as the professionals. It may, however, have positive implications for the arrangements of 'family group conferences' in certain circumstances (Marsh & Crow, 1997). 'Family secrets' may be shared much more widely than in some British families.

Sharing family knowledge with the professionals has been noted as problematic by others; as Channer and Parton (1990) remark 'the reporting of such incidents may be perceived as betrayal of, or disloyalty to, the whole community' (p. 119). There may also be powerful feelings of shame and stigma which inhibit communication with the official world. When one adds to this the experiences of racism which such families may have had, there are formidable difficulties in establishing trusting and effective relationships. However, this all needs to be put in the general context of contemporary British social welfare. Ethnic minorities may be no more distrustful of professionals than white working class people who are gravely disadvantaged and marginalised; social workers, in particular, may be perceived as dangerous.

The above illustrations of sensitive cultural issues, concerning confidentiality, shame or stigma, are simply indications of bridges which have to be built in effective work. They are quite inadequate and superficial in relation to the diverse groups, both recently settled and long established, that form our contemporary society. Even if more detailed was research available, there can be no substitute for the willingness to listen and learn on the part of individual workers. Maitra (1995), for example, gives an interesting example of assumptions one cannot take for granted in working between cultures. One such is 'that cultural rules may not be broken . . . it requires great patience, ingenuity and consultation with bicultural colleagues to discover culturally sanctioned "get out" clauses' (p. 163).

This chapter began with a consideration of the relationships which exist between the nuclear family and wider family networks or community supports and pointed out that there is evidence that these are frequently damaging and unsatisfactory in the lives of families of neglected children, resulting in considerable social isolation. It went on to consider the significance of cultural factors, especially in relation to ethnic minorities, when working with neglectful families. However, in separating these two themes there is a danger of splitting off discussion of cultural factors from the people who mediate them. As children, the adults around us are the purveyors of culture. Therefore, how we feel about them affects the way cultural values are internalised, absorbed, distorted, resisted or rejected.

The discussion about the vital importance of 'cultural competence' would not be complete without reinforcing the particular significance of issues concerning poverty and material deficits in the lives of some families from ethnic minorities. There is evidence that material and environmental deprivation weighs particularly heavily on certain ethnic groups. Ghate and Hazel (2002), whose focus was on 'parenting in poor environments', did not have sufficiently large numbers of such groups in their sample to make statistical generalisations. But it is likely that these groups will be amongst the most vulnerable in relation to such issues as social exclusion, employment opportunities, and availability of family support. Dutt and Phillips (DoH, 2000b, pp. 65–7) briefly address these matters in relation to black children and illustrate how diverse and complex the situation is, even with reference to the overall category of 'black' (albeit with many subdivisions). There is much more work to be done on the financial and material position of families with different ethnic backgrounds and whether this has any particular relevance to families where there is serious neglect. (It may, of course, be that they are no different in this respect from white British families in the same position.)

Conclusion

This chapter has demonstrated that seriously neglectful families usually exist in conditions of quite severe poverty and social isolation. Any specific connections between such neglect and ethnic or cultural child rearing patterns are not evident, but more knowledge is needed to ensure that these issues are better understood ('cultural competence').

Parents

Issues affecting understanding

This chapter is an attempt to get closer to understanding the parents who seriously neglect their children. It is fraught with dangers, partly because the discussion is theoretically and ideologically contentious and, partly and closely linked, because their behaviour to their children raises powerful and sometimes conflicting feelings in those who work with them. The ecological model, which has been put forward as the best way of viewing the problem generally, frees us from the search for 'single causes' of such maltreatment of children. It allows us to see interplay of different factors. Furthermore, sophisticated statistical work, such as that of Ghate and Hazel (2002), makes it possible to show that some factors seem to play a greater part than others in producing family problems. Their large sample, and a kind of statistical telescope, enable some useful generalisations to be made, although their work deals with a much wider range of families than those we are considering here. However, there is a place for the microscope as well as the telescope; for the workers involved, there is a need to get close enough to look for patterns of behaviour which will enable them to plan their interaction purposefully, rather than simply 'reacting' to the situations and crises which are so typical of these cases.

As with all such work, the process engages the worker's feelings as well as his/her thoughts. Those feelings are affected by a range of factors, personal, professional, social and political. Take one example. In a particular case the feelings might be:

- Personal – the sense of despair when nothing seems to help.
- Professional – anxiety lest the workers be found wanting, a 'failure to protect'.
- Social – tensions aroused by intense local antagonism to the family concerned.
- Political – making this work 'count' in a culture of targets and league tables.

Thus, we do not see the parents with clear-eyed objectivity. Whilst this is true, in greater or lesser extent, for all our encounters with others, working with neglectful families is one of the areas of practice in which it is particularly hard to manage the impact it has on workers appropriately.

Somehow, both the American and British literature on this subject leaves us somewhat distanced from the objects of our concern. This research emphasis has been paralleled in practice. Thoburn *et al.* (1995) comment:

'Whilst most analysts of child protection, policies and practice note the importance of considering such variables as the age of the child, the type of maltreatment and the identity of the person allegedly responsible, less attention has been paid to the many dimensions and biographies of those involved as individuals and families rather than abusing families or abused children . . . Professionals so often appeared to become mesmerised by abusive acts or symptoms of neglect or maltreatment and failed to understand the complex nature of the events and interactions leading to it.' (Thoburn *et al.*, pp. 333–4)

Howe (1996) analyses this in depth in his detailed exploration of the reasons for what he describes as 'the analytically more shallow and increasingly performance orientated context of social theories and practices' (p. 77). The extent of this shift of emphasis is powerfully illustrated by turning back to Mattinson and Sinclair's (1979) remarkable book *Mate and Stalemate*. The fieldwork for this took place in London local authorities at the time of the Maria Colwell inquiry in 1973, (DHSS, 1974a), the impact of which was keenly felt. The year of its publication saw the election of the Conservative government and the beginning of what must surely now be seen as a massive onslaught on the values and the competence of the social work profession. The focus and style of *Mate and Stalemate*, which explored marital work with highly disturbed and disorganised families, using four different kinds of theory with psychodynamic origins, might make its publication today unlikely. Yet its general approach (not necessarily accepted uncritically) is precisely what is needed to put living flesh on the dry bones of so much contemporary research.

Politically driven priorities are part of the explanation for this practice vacuum but there are other, deeper factors as well. One reason for what may be described as 'losing the people' in the drive for evidence based research and practice arises from the retreat from the use of theory which was perceived as potentially 'blaming' the people concerned, discussed earlier (Chapter 1). This is particularly relevant to neglect. The post-war history of concern about neglect is instructive. In the 1950s and 1960s the term 'problem family' was commonly used to describe cases which troubled social workers and bore much resemblance to the families we are here considering (Philp, 1963). The term became unacceptable, as awareness of post-war problems of poverty and its attendant stresses was reawakened and the sociological critique of social workers as 'agents of social control' mounted.

The extent and nature of the external difficulties with which poor parents grappled led to a kind of revulsion against 'the diagnosis' of their troubles in terms of their own emotional or psychological difficulties, which seemed to carry with it implications of criticism or censure. In particular, there was a sharp reaction by social workers against classification or generalisation drawn from psychiatric or psychoanalytic sources. In the 1990s, the growing concern and anger amongst such professionals about poverty and disadvantage, about the growth of an 'underclass' (a word which itself engendered ambivalence), strengthened resistance to any analysis of a family's predicament in which external factors were not stressed.

This chapter is based on two premises: first, that we should not seek to understand the problems of neglectful parents solely in terms of external pressures on them, but rather in terms of individual and family dynamics, with external pressures as (often powerful) contributing factors. Second, and most particularly in cases of neglect, our attempt to understand and intervene effectively will need a framework wide enough to encompass a wide range of emotional and psychological considerations. If we fail to adopt such an approach, we find ourselves intellectually and professionally in a blind alley, in which we cannot progress ideas. However, this attempt is not without difficulties and dangers. These issues are caught up in the cross-currents of ideological differences, of social scientific dispute and of professional rivalries, leaving the less experienced workers unsupported and exposed. They are also extremely complex, especially if one wishes to be pragmatic and eclectic, taking from different theories or areas of knowledge what seems to be useful. Yet this may be exactly the best way; as Jung put it: 'One could as little catch the psyche in a theory as one could the world. Theories are not articles of faith; they are either instruments of knowledge and or therapy or they are no good at all' (Jung, 1993).

Since the Labour government came into power in 1997, policies concerning families who are defined as problematic in their behaviour towards others and in the upbringing of their children have become much more explicit. The professionals concerned have been drawn into a variety of interventions as a result of these policies. Families who are described as 'socially excluded' include a number of those with which this book is concerned. The presenting characteristics of both parents and children are well known to social workers. These are families who are 'troublesome' to professionals and neighbours, the parents' care of their children is patently inadequate in many aspects, and the families have been shown to be very, very hard to help. The model presented here and the discussion of poverty and isolation will, I hope, reassure the reader that due weight is given to external stressors. Whatever the academic tensions between what might loosely be called a 'sociological' or 'psychological' view of such parents' difficulties, however uncertain workers may be about using terms or descriptions which might further stigmatise families, the fact remains that when such workers come together, they recognise something that is distinctive about the difficulties, which makes these neglectful families stand out from others in similar material circumstances. The evidence is based on practice experience and wisdom. 'We know one when we see one.' We do no service to the families if we reject our intuitive knowledge.

So what are the parents like?

To adapt a comment made about the child by Lord Justice Butler-Sloss (1988) 'the parent is a person, not an object for concern' (p. 245). They laugh and they cry; they are generous and mean; they are fat and thin (and occasionally medium); they are busy and they are lazy. Those social workers who have formed long-term working relationships with such parents retain vivid and distinctive memories about them after many years. Furthermore, although much of this chapter will be devoted to characteristics and issues which perplex and worry us, we also recognise that for some against whom all the dice have been loaded since birth, mere survival seems a triumph. However, the sympathy which is aroused by such awareness may itself be a problem, if it leads us away from the primary task – to ensure the well-being of their children.

What do we know about the characteristics of these parents?

Background history

Gaudin's (1993) summary of current knowledge about neglect (see Chapter 1) identifies a number of critical dimensions. The first of these concerns the developmental history of the parents themselves. It will come as no surprise to practitioners to learn that many neglectful parents grew up in unstable, hostile, non-nurturing homes, which led to unstable personalities when the children became adults, which in turn led to stressful marriages and abusive parenting practices towards children (p. 12).

Gaudin also draws attention to the value of attachment theory in understanding the effects of past events on parenting capacity. This body of theory has been the subject of extensive general research and scrutiny on both sides of the Atlantic. (These issues will be explored further in the next chapter on the children.) Rigorous examination by, amongst others, Rutter and Rutter (1993) led to a conclusion in which we can have confidence:

> 'It seems that the postulate that a lack of continuity in the loving committed parent child relationships is central has received substantial support. What has stood the test of time most of all has been the proposition that the quality of parent child relationships constitutes a central aspect of parenting, that the development of social relationships occupies a crucial role in personality growth and that abnormalities in relationships are important in many types of psychopathology.' (Rutter & Rutter, pp. 341 and 361)

Others have examined neglectful parents specifically in this theoretical context, notably Egeland (1988a; b), and have found connections between unstable attachments in childhood and later parenting difficulties. However, the nature of these connections is (and perhaps will always be) somewhat uncertain, as is the evidence on the notion of intergenerational 'cycles' of neglect, in which the debates are strikingly similar to those concerning 'cycles of deprivation' in the 1970s and 1980s (Fuller & Stevenson, 1983). Whilst, as Gaudin (1993) points out, numerous studies do suggest a cycle of neglect, 'the direct cause–effect relationship between parental history of neglect and subsequent neglect of children is not clearly established' (p. 13). Indeed, the uncertainty leads us to a less deterministic view of human nature, as well as a recognition of what Gaudin describes as 'important mediating factors': 'Victims of neglect who do not repeat the cycle have fewer stressful life events; stronger, more stable and supportive relationships with husbands and boyfriends; physically healthier babies.' They are also 'less likely to be maltreated by both parents and more apt to have reported a supportive relationship with one parent or with another adult. *These mediating factors provide critical indicators for improving parents' potential'* (p. 13).

The message from the research, then, is reasonably clear. On the one hand, it makes no sense (in fact it is nonsense) to divorce the past from the present in reflection about the experiences of neglectful parents, especially in their childhood. Indeed, 'personal identities and a sense of belonging form within our relationship history' (Howe, 1997). On the other hand, many recent or present experiences, whether in relationships or in life events or situations, may tip the balance one way or another. Such a conclusion is vague but that vagueness is at once both more hopeful and more important than definitive links, for it affirms the necessity for those working with the families, first, to look for connections between past and present which are meaningful to the individuals concerned, for example, a mother's perception that she was not cherished as a child has a more direct bearing on work with her than 'the facts' of her deprivation. Second, it encourages a model of work which seeks to build on recent and present strengths and good experiences in the confidence that they can make a difference.

Not surprisingly, studies of neglectful parents have also highlighted a range of characteristics which have been described in terms of personality traits. However, Pianti *et al.* (1989), in their review of aetiological factors in child maltreatment, comment that:

> 'Recently, investigations have turned to examining parental characteristics that are more directly tied to mothers' thoughts and feelings about caretaking rather than measuring static personality traits . . . which at best may have only a hypothetical link to caretaking skills . . . These studies have begun to demonstrate rather consistently that one characteristic differentiating maltreating from adequate caretakers is their lack of understanding of the complexity of social relationships, especially caretaking and their feelings about meeting the needs of another person.' (Pianti *et al.*, 1989, p. 205)

Pianti *et al.* are not here specifically examining neglect, but maltreatment more generally. Other studies have found, however, that neglectful mothers lack knowledge of, and empathy for, children's age appropriate needs and have more unrealistic and more negative expectations of their children than non-neglecting parents (Jones & McNeely, 1980). Thus, the direct line between the past and the present would seem to be reinforced. It raises important questions as to whether and how such difficulties can be addressed. We shall return to this in later chapters.

Low self-esteem is pervasive in the descriptions of women who neglect their children. Although low self-esteem is a feature of depression, it can exist without the conventional signs of depression. Whilst many factors can and do contribute in adult life to this poor rating of oneself, some neglectful mothers convey a powerful sense that they have not been cherished or nurtured themselves in their formative years. Every dimension of care for the self may be affected by this. Their life story seems to be:

'If I am not loved, then I am not worthy of love. It follows that there is no point in seeking to make myself attractive to others, either through appearance or responses. Even my house can be dirty like me; my children, who are, after all, bits of me, need not (cannot) be cherished. As for men, they are allowed to exploit me; maybe because this is how men always were in my family and because I do not deserve anything better.'

It will, of course, not always be as bleak or pervasive as that. But the worker has to make the leap of imagination, based on, and informed by, clear observation, to feel the despair and hopelessness which lies in the hearts of some neglectful mothers. It is essential for realistic, as well as compassionate, strategies to raise self-esteem. Without it, in such cases, the endless cycle of advice, practical aid, 'sending in the dirty squad to clean up', is doomed to failure. Meanwhile, the children suffer grievously.

The responses of mothers to young children

However, important as the deeper reason for low self-esteem may be in certain cases, it is frequently reinforced by 'failure' in the here and now. That failure has been described in terms of a deficit in social skills. In relation to the care of children, this may suggest a different model for understanding which has been interestingly explored by Crittenden (1993). She argues that:

'Although neglect clearly results from a nested hierarchy of influences (including social, ecological, family, dyadic attachment), knowledge of internal processes leading to the failure to respond may provide essential information regarding neglectful behaviour.' (Crittenden, 1993, p. 28)

Crittenden seeks to integrate developmental theory with cognitive theory and groups neglectful parents in terms of how they perceive, interpret and respond to information. She claims that in the approach 'major theoretical perspectives that are often treated as competing are viewed as complementary . . . Normative processes, typical of humans, are applied to the case of neglect' (p. 28). She argues that, although these distinctions may seem a long way from the usual concerns about neglectful parents' omissions, an understanding of the parents' style of processing information directly contributes to their ability:

(1)   To perceive essential aspects of their children's states.
(2)   To interpret accurately the meaning of these perceptions.

(3) To select adaptive responses.
(4) To respond in ways which meet the children's needs. (Crittenden, 1993, p. 29)

Crittenden believes that they may experience reality differently from other parents on any of these dimensions. If this is so, 'simply instructing neglectful parents may be ineffective' (p. 30).

This way of observing mother–child interactions would seem to have particular value when the children are very young. Crittenden's illustration deals with the responses to crying babies. She shows that, in the first stage of processing, the crying may appear simply not to be heard – 'throwing away the stimulus information'. In the second stage, meaning must be interpreted – what kind of crying is this? (Mothers naturally distinguish between different cries of their infants.) In the third, a response must be selected: what can be done about it? This involves believing one can take effective action. In the fourth, the response must be implemented, which depends on a range of immediate circumstances and the parent's capacity to meet the child's needs rather than their own (pp. 30–31).

Crittenden develops each of these stages in terms of the particular difficulties of neglectful parents, linking this to existing research. Most importantly, she discusses the implications for treatment. Her approach has been considered here in some detail, not simply for its intrinsic, substantive interest but because it shows a way of sharpening up the individual observations which must lie at the root of useful assessment. It also emphasises the interactional nature of parent–child ties, an issue which has also been extensively explored by Mass (1996), who writes:

'Parenting is inherently interpersonal, a person is a parent only in relation to another. Nevertheless, the parental experience, in particular the experience of parents of infants, has been conventionally defined as an intrapersonal, not as an interpersonal phenomenon.' (Mass, 1996, p. 425)

Once it is accepted that from birth the infant is capable of entering into two-way communication, an observation can be based on interactional behaviour. Mass examines the causes that parents attribute to the behaviour of their child. For example, there can be attributions which are made to the infant's characteristics or to his intentions. 'He was a premature baby. All premature babies cry a lot.' Or, 'He cries to irritate me.' Mass's work is conceptually complex and cannot be explored here in depth but, as with Crittenden, it opens the door on present interaction as a basis for understanding the situations in neglectful families. As children grow older, the power of interactional factors becomes more readily apparent. The work described here, however, enables 'signals' of parent–child dynamics to be picked up at a very early stage. In cases of neglect, this may be of particular importance.

Thus far, then, in seeking to understand neglectful parents, we have moved from consideration of links between past and present to a range of ways in which the present situation may be viewed.

Typologies of neglectful parents

Crittenden (1999) has proposed a model for understanding neglectful parents in which there are three different groups. She is tentative and acknowledges that there is as yet no clear evidence for such typologies. However, it is valuable to have put before us a possible way of differentiating between parents who are characterised as neglectful.

Crittenden identifies three types of neglect which she describes as 'disorganised'; 'depressed' and 'emotionally neglecting'. Tying her argument to the question of how humans process information, which was discussed above, she picks out 'cognition' and 'affect' as two elements of information. 'Cognition is information about what actions effectively cause specific outcomes . . . about the effects of one's behaviour'. Affect is 'information about the safety or dangers of contexts', that is, 'feeling states' that motivate a range of behaviours, including those concerned with protection and affection (p. 51).

Of the three types of family described, the first 'the disorganised' is the one most immediately recognisable to those who work in or with children's services. Crittenden headlines them as 'Living from crisis to crisis: defending against cognition' and allowing affect to be dominant. She gives a vivid and instantly recognisable account of such families. 'Being in their homes is a confusing, frustrating experience . . . because . . . there are constant interruptions' (p. 52). 'Feelings motivate behaviour; that is, family members organise their behaviour in terms of how they feel. Under these conditions, a professional's time and resources may be hijacked to meet the mother's priorities' (p. 52–53), which are usually the most immediate and the most intense. 'The family is always on the verge of disaster' (p. 55).

The description which Crittenden gives is compelling in its familiarity, and the consequences of the behaviours upon the family's functioning and, in particular, on the children's development are very grave. A wide range of professionals become involved in the parents' chaotic journeys through daily life, the parents are usually the object of heavy criticism, even vilification, in the neighbourhood. Sometimes, but not always, such parents come from similarly disorganised backgrounds and seem to have had no other models of family life. It is, however, important to distinguish between limitation of intellect which may make it difficult to cope with the complex demands of bringing up children and the overwhelming power of emotions (or affect) which, as it were, swamp intellect in an urgent need for instant responses or solutions. It is the latter which Crittenden describes. Later in this chapter we shall consider the former – the position of parents with learning disabilities.

Crittenden's second type of parental behaviour, 'depressed neglect' may be less immediately familiar to social workers in child protection, but is well worth careful reflection in the process of assessment. She describes them as:

> 'Defending against both affect and cognition. The individuals in these families are withdrawn and dull. They do not seem motivated to work for their children's benefit. This is not because they do not love their children – they do. It is that they do not perceive their children's needs, even after we have explained them. In addition, they do not believe that anything we do, or that they could do, will change the situation. They are ... passive and helpless.' (Crittenden, 1999, pp. 62–63)

Crittenden suggests that 'although this is similar to ordinary depression, [it] may actually be a more profound state.' She relates this to the concept of 'learned helplessness' described by Seligman (1975) and points out that this depression has been found to be associated with children's neglect (Zuravin & Diblasio, 1996). The typology used by Crittenden offers a way of identifying those parents whose lives are blighted by a kind of pervasive despair, where they have no sense of control over their destiny. They may present some of the same external characteristics as the 'disorganised parents', for example, the children's lack of hygiene, chronic late attendance at school, non-attendance at health appointments and so on. But for constructive interventions, the difference between 'disorganised' and 'depressed' may be important.

Crittenden's third type of parental behaviour is described as 'emotional neglect – emotional poverty in the land of plenty: defending against affect' (p. 57). This takes us into less familiar territory for child protection social workers but more familiar for workers in Child and Mental Health Services (CAMHS). The term 'emotional abuse' encompasses such behaviours. 'The failure to connect emotionally with others is at the heart of emotional neglect' (p. 57). These are well-organised, highly structured households, with material comforts and advantages; there is nothing wrong with their cognition. However, 'human relationships become defined by performance and affect is suppressed' (p. 58.) Although these family situations are distressing and extremely destructive to children's mental health and well-being, they are not dealt with here in the depth which they deserve. This is because the objective of this book is to progress our thinking about the 'disorganised' and the 'depressed', who at present form the core of the intractable and worrying cases in child protection. The impact on children of these particular parental behaviours will be discussed in the next chapter.

Gender

Farmer and Owen (1995) point out that, in their study, 'the focus on mothers pervaded all aspects of the child protection system' (p. 319). They rightly remind us that this is despite the fact that in sexual and physical abuse men play the major part. However, it is women, usually the mothers, who are pivotal in cases of neglect. They suggest that whether the abuse was committed by a man or a woman, the focus of responsibility was on the women, 'who were seen as more amenable and available for intervention' (p. 319). They describe the focus on mothers as 'relentless' and urge that the risks to children should be 'disaggregated' so that practitioners take more account of the particular person from whom a child is at risk (p. 319). They also comment that: 'In most cases of neglect and emotional abuse there was a general assumption that mothers were responsible for all deficits in the case' (p. 318). In view of the numbers of such households which are headed by a lone mother, this is inevitable, but the factors underlying it and the implications for practice merit careful examination. Since the first edition of this book, various British authors have taken further the issue of gender in child maltreatment, including neglect (Featherstone, 1999; 2001). Practitioners can now be clearer about the ethical and sociological questions surrounding current practice and can use this understanding for more effective assessment and intervention.

There are four issues at the centre of the debate. These are: changes in family structures; care and mothering as 'women's work'; the rights, responsibilities and roles of fathers in the family; dangerous men and vulnerable mothers.

Changes in family structures

Daniel and Taylor (2005) point out that:

> 'The circumstances of children involved in child protection processes in Britain are different . . . from the majority of children. Although there is a rise (generally) in the number of lone parent families, abused and neglected children are far more likely to be with one parent than the norm. So whilst 73% of children in the UK live with both parents and 8% in reconstituted families, only 38% of those involved in the child protection process live with both parents.' (Ryan & Little, 2000)

Most of the lone parents in child protection cases are mothers. In cases of neglect, when there are fathers they tend to be unemployed and the families are usually living in extremely deprived circumstances. Practitioners will also have noted that in families headed by a lone mother in which children are seriously neglected, it is not uncommon to find 'serial men', who come and go in the life of the family; some have fathered some of the children.

Thus, the family structures in such cases mirror but also magnify the radical change in British society generally. To look back at Philp's book, *Family Failure*, published in 1963, is to be reminded of the extent and pace of this phenomenon. Philp's 'problem families', to use the terminology of the time, were, characteristically, headed by married couples. Our contemporary reality means that workers engaged with neglectful families will usually be working directly only with mothers. This is why the other three issues to be outlined here are so important.

Care and mothering as 'women's work'

In the literature referred to above, which examines 'care and mothering', there is important debate about the idealised expectations which are held in society generally of women and their maternal role. There has been deep reluctance to acknowledge the ambivalence which exists in women about motherhood. Turney (2005), in asking the question: 'Women and neglect: why does it matter?' (pp. 256–7) makes the following trenchant points:

- It leads to the personalising or individualising of the very complex problem of neglect and to the pathologising of women . . . Then it is easy to slip into a mother-blaming approach.
- A gender-biased approach runs the risk of producing only partial assessments.' (Men are not 'in the picture'.)
- Acknowledgement of the diversity of individual women's feelings about motherhood is necessary to assess and intervene effectively.

The rights, responsibilities and roles of fathers in the family

There is much debate about the role of fathers in contemporary society. It is an issue which arises in many different contexts, for example, in relation to finance and to fathers' rights in courts of law. There are also underlying theoretical debates about the part they play in child rearing. For example, how far are they 'interchangeable' with mothers as attachment figures? Do they have distinctively masculine attributes, important for children's psychological development and as role models?

Although such considerations are relevant to the understanding of any family, the situation in most seriously neglectful families is often complicated by fundamental doubts about fathers' influence on, and behaviour towards, the women and children whom they live with, often transiently. However, it remains true that the potentiality for positive engagement of fathers in their children's lives has been little explored in child protection practice, or, indeed, more widely in child welfare. They are more often seen in negative terms.

Dangerous men and vulnerable families

It is important to be open to the possibility of positive work to help men relate more effectively to their families. It remains, however, sadly true that a significant number of seriously neglectful families have connections with men, in or out of the household, who pose a grave threat to children. This goes beyond the 'omissions' of care which characterise neglect and arises in part from the vulnerability of these mothers and children to abuse. Thus, physical and sexual violence to the woman and her children is often part of the situation. Unfortunately, practitioners do not always appreciate the seriousness of this, either because the mother and children are silenced, or, in the case of some sexual abuse, generational boundaries are confused. Furthermore, the dangerousness of some men is fuelled by drug or alcohol misuse.

What, then, are we to conclude about the relevance of gender to our understanding of parenting in cases of neglect? To avoid the 'mother blaming' which is so often aroused by the situations of lone, neglectful mothers, there has to be an acceptance that women generally vary in their wish and capacity to assume the responsibilities ascribed to them. It is interesting to reflect on the type of mother described by Crittenden (1999) as 'emotionally neglectful', who has the cognitive capacity and the material resources to make other arrangements for the care of children to whom she cannot readily respond maternally. Some mothers are 'disorganised' or dominated by the emotions of the moment, but this does not mean that they are less ambivalent about motherhood. Mothers may be depressed in part because this is a role they do not want. The message for managers and workers, in seeking to formulate a care plan, is that they should not collude with idealised assumptions about this. They should be prepared to contemplate the possibility that some women do not want to be mothers. The children are ill served by a refusal to accept this, difficult as the journeys through 'the system' and the courts will be.

However, ambivalence rather than outright rejection will more often be apparent to the workers. In such circumstances, important questions arise as to whether the negative feelings about motherhood can be explored and constructive plans made on the basis that 'there is more to life than motherhood'. To lift the low self-esteem which is so often apparent in these mothers may lead to a more positive acceptance of the mothering role. (This raises issues about women's employment and of the acquisition of skills, outside the home.)

This recognition of the uncertainties surrounding the state and meaning of motherhood is important because it allows the women we are here considering the dignity of being the same as others and avoids the scapegoating which is so common. Nonetheless, and even more important, the ecological model at the heart of this book affords a more comprehensive rebuttal of the 'mother blaming' culture, for it reminds us that such women may be caught up in a complex web of factors, internal and external, which taken together can produce situations in which they are seemingly hopelessly entangled. They are not reluctant mothers; they are desperate people. Part of the work to be done is to free them from some of the strands of the web in which they are caught.

What of the fathers or the men involved in caring? The message is more cautious. It is absolutely clear that, in child welfare generally, the position of fathers and the possibilities of working more constructively require more positive attention. It is less clear whether the men who are usually involved with seriously neglectful mothers are those with whom positive engagement is likely to be possible. There will of course, be exceptions, as, for example, some couples who are both learning disabled. But there has to be careful appraisal of risk, some of it hidden, as, for example, when men use families of this kind to groom children for sexual abuse.

Thus, the parent who will usually be the most important or only significant person in the lives of these children will be the mother. Her feelings about the role must be explored if apparent deficits are to be understood. Awareness of the role of men in her life, who may or may not be the fathers of the children, and the patterns of their interactions, is crucial to a care plan.

Substance abuse, depression, and learning disability

Thus far, we have considered the links between the past and present and the issue of gender as it impacts on the families. It is obvious that such parents, like everyone else, may experience a range of mental disorders; workers with these particular families will need to seek expert advice as these occur. However, it seems, from the experience of practitioners, that one aspect of parental mental health, substance abuse, whether of drugs or alcohol, looms very large.

The other issue to be discussed in this section relates to parents with learning disabilities, which poses particular difficulties in cases of neglect. This chapter does not discuss parental disabilities of other kinds. There is ample evidence (Olsen & Wates, 2003) that disabled parents who become involved in child protection processes do not receive appropriate support. However, the existence of a physical disability in the parent does not raise the same problems for the care of children as occurs when the behaviour of a parent towards a child is affected by mental disorder or learning disability. Of course, the needs of physically disabled parents for sensitive and sophisticated help, underpinned by a model of social inclusion, is essential in child welfare work. If children are found to be in severe, chronic neglect in such cases, it means either that there are other factors involved or that there has been a deplorable lack of imagination and competence by service providers.

Drug abuse

Since the first edition of this book was published, the extent and gravity of the problem which drug-abusing parents pose has been more fully recognised and documented. There is also much concern that the issue of alcohol abuse should not be overlooked.

In 2004, the Advisory Council on the Misuse of Drugs reported to the government on 'the needs of children of problem drug users' (ACMD, 2004). The report covered the whole of the UK, although there are important differences regionally. For our purposes, the following is of particular importance.

- The report is focused on those parents whose drug abuse poses risks for the care of their children. It does not assume that *all* such parents pose such problems.
- To arrive at an estimate of risk, a profile was created as follows:

  Drug use risk factors:
  – daily heroin use
  – daily alcohol use with use of illicit drugs
  – regular stimulant use
  – sharing of injecting equipment
  Social risk factors:
  – unstable accommodation
  – living alone or with strangers
  – living with another drug user
  – criminal justice involvement.

- The report estimates that there are between 200 000 and 300 000 children of problem drug users in England and Wales, i.e. about

2–3% of the ten million children aged under 16. In Scotland, they conclude that between 40 880 and 58 700 children are in this position, i.e. about 4–6% of the one million children.

- In the years between 1996–2000, there was a dramatic increase in the numbers of parents with such problems, both those whose children were living with them and those with children living away. (Table 1.4 from *Hidden Harm*, ACDM, 2004, shows an increase from about 7000 in 1996 to about 22 000 in 2000.)
- During this period (1996–2000), about half of these children were living away from their parents. However, only a small proportion of them (about 5%) were in care. (ACDM, 2004 p. 23)

Behind these bald figures lies a social problem of some magnitude. Whilst not all the children at risk would be categorised as 'neglected', the maltreatment which they experience is highly likely to include neglect as a most significant factor. Our holistic understanding of the concept of neglect means that these 'omissions' of care may affect all aspects of children's development and well-being. Thus, the deficits are not simply in physical or health matters but in lack of emotional responsiveness, ('you were not there for me') and failure to protect children from the dangerous outside world of the drug dealers and those who accompany them. Sadly, the figures show that about half of these children were already living away from their parents. It is interesting that only a small proportion were in care or 'looked after'. Others were cared for by relatives or friends. The report notes that 'losing a parent through separation or death is much more common for the children of drug users than other children' (p. 36). Death from infections such as HIV or hepatitis B or C is an additional hazard.

There is now substantial evidence, especially from the USA, of the harm caused to children by parental substance abuse and by neglect (Dubowitz, 1999). This, of course, raises complex questions about the relationship between the two; there are multiple factors associated with neglectful parenting and it is exceedingly difficult, if not impossible, to disentangle the significance of drug use from other factors. However, for responsible practitioners, it may be enough to examine and analyse, case by case, asking the question: 'In what ways does substance abuse appear to be adversely affecting the care of the children?' Often, the answers will be obvious and are not unique to this particular problem. Cleaver *et al.* (1999) set out the ways in which mental illness, problem drug use or domestic violence may affect parenting and the likely effects on children's development. However, there are some aspects of drug misuse which merit particular note.

First, there is the possibility that neglectful parents may tip the scales towards substance abuse in their children, young people or adults. Dunn *et al.* (2002), in a tightly argued and intricate study, suggest that 'available evidence indicates that children who experience paren-tal neglect, with or without parental alcohol or drug abuse, are at high risk of substance use disorder (SUD). The effects of parental substance abuse on the substance abuse outcomes of their children appear to be partly mediated by their neglectful parenting' (p. 1). Clearly, such an argument is more plausible when families live in localities where drug misuse is prevalent.

Murphy *et al.* (1991) cogently point out, in relation to substance abuse generally:

'Although substance abuse may be only one of many problems in these families, it is one which can be identified and, sometimes, treated successfully . . . The converse may be even more impor-tant . . . unless this problem is identified or treated, there is very little point in beginning other forms of treatment.' (Murphy *et al.*, 1991, p. 209)

Thus, there are three reasons why particular attention should be paid to substance abuse in neglectful families. First, there is substantial evidence from the UK and the USA that the problem is widespread and has a very damaging effect on children's development. Second, without specific intervention on this issue, other interventions are less likely to be successful. Third, it is possible that the children will them-selves by drawn into substance abuse as young people or adults.

In Chapter 5, we shall consider the roles of different workers in rela-tion to neglectful families. The special expertise of drug action teams and medical advisors are an essential part of the teamwork. However, it is also necessary for other workers to be reasonably well informed, especially those who are tasked with making an assessment of child safety. One important element in this knowledge is the likely effect of particular substances on parental behaviour and competence; without this, the assessment may be unrealistic, negatively or posi-tively. Thus, the main types of drugs and their effects should be distinguished: heroin or other opiates, cocaine and amphetamine, ben-zodiazepine, tobacco and cannabis, and alcohol. Of course, these may be varyingly combined. There is also the question of blood borne viruses, particularly HIV, hepatitis C or B (ACMD, 2004, pp. 32–3). Adams (1999) in a study of social workers in the London area found that they were ill-informed about the effectiveness of methadone on parenting adequacy. In general, there are important implications for better knowledge on the part of workers in child protection.

In recent years the impact of substance abuse upon the unborn child has been better documented (Chasnof & Lowder, 1999; ACMD, 2004; Walker & Glasgow, 2005). ACMD (2004) usefully, if dep discuss this issue (pp. 31–2). They point out that 'drugs can the foetus at any time during the pregnancy, causing a wide range of abnormalities'. However, to assess the effects of drugs on the foetus 'becomes virtually impossible when the mother is using several drugs in varying quantities and her general health and diet is poor'. Nonetheless, following prolonged exposure to opiates or benzodiazepine in pregnancy, there are certain specific symptoms in newborn babies, such as irritability and constant crying, which are well documented. The transmission of blood viruses to the baby *in utero* is also established, although recent advances in treatment make this treatable, if the diagnosis is made.

In the next chapter, on children, some of the specific effects on their development when parents abuse drugs will be considered, together with children's resistance and coping capacity. Some of the advice offered by Murphy and Harbin (2003) on assessment is to be found at Appendix 4. Adams' (1999) study suggests that social workers were ambivalent towards parents who abused drugs and uncertain as to the extent to which they could be helped to parent more effectively. The large majority agreed that 'trying to help drug using parents is a worthwhile task' and that they 'are capable of changing drug abusing behaviour'. However, this positive approach was qualified by other responses. There is a need for much more evidence on this, but, so far, the burden of the evidence both from research and from the experience of practitioners clearly shows that 'parental drug abuse has the potential to interfere with virtually all aspects of a child's health and development' (ACDM, 2004, p. 41).

Alcoholism

The effects of drug abuse on parenting has of late received more attention than the effects of alcoholism. We have already noted that both may be present in some of the cases we are considering. Many of the same problems in the care of children arise in both situations; both result in a degree of self-absorption in which the needs of the parent take precedence over the needs of the child. However, despite longstanding evidence of the effects of alcoholism on individuals and families, and the present concern over sharp rises in alcohol consumption in the UK, there has been surprisingly little discussion of alcohol misuse in relation to child maltreatment, specifically neglect. (There has been more awareness of its connections with domestic violence.)

As with drugs, there is clear evidence on the adverse effects of alcohol on the unborn child (Cleaver *et al.*, 1999). It is also self-evident that heavy intake of alcohol can lead to neglectful parenting, which carries a high level of risk, especially in relation to infants and toddlers. Less well understood may be the impact on children's emotional well-being when parents are preoccupied and unavailable. This is sensitively described by Christensen (1997), who reported on a small qualitative study:

> 'Children always knew of the parents' alcohol abuse years before the parent realised they did . . . Children are afraid of being abandoned. They are afraid that their parents will die (they may often have seen them appear lifeless in a coma from drinking) . . . They are afraid that other people will find out . . . with the result that they themselves will be branded what they term a 'loser.' (Christensen, 1997, pp. 28–29)

In such family situations, especially when it is the mother who is alcohol dependent, family patterns and roles can become distorted, such as when children assume adult roles to care for their mother and other siblings. (I recall the experience of a social worker visiting such a family and knocking on the door. She heard the three-year-old girl say 'be a good girl and open the door' to her mother.)

Dube *et al.* (2001) provide some statistical evidence of the impact of these problems on children. Their study in the USA (a large sample) is a detailed examination of the association between parental alcohol abuse and various forms of childhood abuse, neglect and household dysfunction. These factors (ten in number) are called 'adverse childhood experiences' (ACEs). They found 'strong relationships between parental alcohol abuse and all ACEs' (p. 9). In a sample of about four and a half thousand women and nearly four thousand men, about 10% suffered physical neglect and nearly 15% suffered emotional neglect (p. 9). However, it is worth noting that other ACEs, such as physical and sexual abuse ranked considerably higher. Domestic violence directed at the mother, with its effects on children, loomed large.

In summary: the fact that substance abuse, of either kind, is a major concern in so many seriously neglectful parents and that it impinges on so many aspects of their children's lives, above all when their addiction leads to antisocial patterns of living and/or escalating debt, justifies particular emphasis in this chapter. There is little evidence that parents whose addiction is controlled, for example, by methadone, cope more satisfactorily, though this seems a reasonable hypothesis. Where addiction is uncontrolled, this problem so distorts parenting behaviour that, in the range of complex factors associated with the ecological model, early and energetic action on this should take precedence.

Maternal depression

We have earlier discussed Crittenden's suggestion that depression may be a distinguishing factor in the typologies of neglectful parents.

However, even if that model is not followed, the problem of depression is so important that it merits special consideration.

The extent, nature and pervasiveness of this aspect of the human condition is well recognised. There is broad agreement that social and environmental factors play an important part in depression and it is therefore likely to be significant in the families with whom we are concerned. However, the relationship between depression and child maltreatment, including neglect, is not very well understood. Cleaver *et al.* (1999) point out that they failed to find a link in the literature between 'the possible association between parental mental illness and the type of child abuse' (p. 14).

We are on rather firmer ground when we seek to understand better the likely impact on the interactions of parent and child when the former is depressed and to consider, in particular, the issue of neglect. Cleaver *et al.* (1999) identify a number of ways in which parenting can be affected by depression. They consider the following and give examples:

- Parenting skills: 'apathy and listlessness, classic symptoms of depression . . . mean parents have difficulty in organising their lives' (p. 32).
- Perception: 'mental illness . . . can result in parents having a warped view of the world . . . Research suggests that depressed mothers see themselves as inferior . . . less competent and adequate than non-depressed mothers' (p. 33).
- Control and emotion: 'depression can also make parents irritable and angry with children' (p. 33).
- Neglect and physical needs: 'for some mothers [in violent relationships] there were periods of despair. "For about a year . . . I didn't give a shit about how the children looked"' (p. 34).
- Attachment: major depression can *inter alia* cause mothers:

  - 'To be insensitive to their children's needs'
  - 'To be unresponsive to their cues' (p. 35).

- The effects of depression on the processes of attachment are of particular importance.

For practitioners, who frequently encounter depression in the parents of children at risk, there is a need to see some of the complex factors at play and consider their interventions on this basis. For example, in addition to the importance of ensuring that appropriate medication is provided, the social and environmental issues must also be taken into account. In a complex but powerful discussion of a study of child abuse and maternal depression, Sheppard (1997) asserts that:

'It must be recognised that these data provide extensive evidence for an important link between child abuse and depression . . . Maternal depression was indeed associated with severely problematic circumstances . . . The "double jeopardy" of abuse and depression . . . was noticeably associated with particular factors . . . These were associated most closely with the number of children, the lack of basic amenities, overcrowding, and absence of earned income and employment . . . They are also distinctively associated with problems in the provision of positive affect towards their children, poor guidance of the child and unrealistic expectations of their children.' (Sheppard, 1997, p. 103)

In summary: chronic, pervasive depression in a parent (usually a mother) who seriously neglects her children may not be seen for what it is when it is overlaid by a plethora of daily problems and traumatic events. To investigate the possibility can take us behind presenting behaviour and symptoms to a deeper level of understanding.

Parents with learning disabilities

Finally, in the consideration of 'parenting', I turn to the growing interest in the relationship (if such there be) between the presence of learning disabilities in parents and their capacity to parent, most particularly to offer care and supervision which is 'good enough'. Here we enter an ideological minefield. The stigmatising, inappropriate and inhumane treatment of generations of people believed to have a degree of learning disability, in which there were many whose apparent mental disability resulted from gross social deprivation and/or physical and sensory problems, is well known. It is a source of shame to an older generation of professionals and fuels a worthy determination in younger workers that such people should have every opportunity to lead an ordinary family life with their children. The tales which recur, of 'eugenics', of institutionalisation, of sterilisation in the not too distant past, further reinforce such determination. In social work education, students are now much more engaged by the idea of work with people with learning difficulties and frequently come to professional training with experience in this field.

There has been a sea change in the attitudes of many professionals generally to the rights of people with learning disabilities to have and bring up children. This is in the context of wider cultural shifts towards the concept of human right and social justice for all disabled people. The fact that there is now much more debate about such issues and a powerful critique of public services for disabled people reflects this increased awareness and the growing effectiveness of advocacy by, and on behalf of, this group of citizens. Their silence has been broken. It is perverse not to acknowledge this, although the realisation of the ideal still falls short of 'good enough' practice in many instances. The inspection report by Goodringe (DoH, 2000) on *Services to Support Disabled Adults in their Parenting Role* provides a balanced account of the position in England a few years ago. However, Olsen and Wates (2003), in a full review of the literature, found major deficits.

With regard to parents with a learning disability and their care of children, the situation appears to be even more polarised than when the first edition of this book was written. In simple terms, there is a gulf between those whose primary focus is to seek justice (as they see it) for such parents and those whose primary focus is the protection of the children. In the professional and academic literature, the criticisms of the services offered have intensified since 1998 (for example: Booth & Booth, 1999; 2003; Olsen & Wates, 2003; Tarleton *et al.*, 2006). Those representing children's services have not responded vigorously to the criticisms. Yet it is obvious to those in touch with the field that there are a significant number of such families who cause anxiety because their care of the children falls below 'good enough' standards.

One of the most disturbing aspects of this debate is the evidence, cited most recently by Tarleton *et al.*, that a disproportionate number of the children of learning disabled parents do not live with their parents. 'It is . . . clear that parents with learning difficulties are far more likely than other parents to have their children removed from them and permanently placed outside the home' (p. 1). The UK national survey (Emerson *et al.*, 2005) found that 48% of such parents were not looking after their own children (p. 1). However, it is not clear in the UK survey how many such children were in 'State care' and how many were informally cared for by relatives. McConnell and Llewellyn (2002), in an international review, have made a valuable exploration of the unusually high rate at which children of parents with learning disabilities are removed from their care. They report that a number of different studies have found removal rates between 40–60%. The focus of their article is on the evidence as to how 'parents with intellectual disability fare in child protection and court proceedings' (p. 298). They conclude that 'allegations of child abuse being perpetrated' by such parents are 'quite rare' but they point out that 'concerns about neglect (serious omissions of care) are the most common form of concern raised' (p. 301). This, of course, is what makes the issue so important in the context of this book. British practitioners in the child protection field will recognise that there is a subgroup of neglectful parents in which the question of intellectual competence looms large.

However, the authors point out that, within this group, there is also a high prevalence of medical and psychiatric problems, and often a history of deprivation and social disadvantage. This is unsurprising and reinforces the complexity of the 'ecological model' – intellectual disability is likely to be but one of the factors which contribute to the problem. They also argue, persuasively, that stereotyped views of such parents may result in unfair and discriminating legal processes. This tightly argued and wide-ranging article is an important addition to the debate.

Tarleton *et al.* suggest that 'the conventional assumption has been that the intellectual limitation of the parents will, almost inevitably, lead to adverse outcomes for the child. Booth and Booth (1993) mounted a strong case for professionals to review their approach. They drew attention to the many other factors, both intra- and interpersonal and environmental, which affect parental competence. They argued that these factors are as significant in child maltreatment amongst parents with learning disabilities as they are in other groups and that therefore attention to these problems will be as, or more pertinent, than focusing on their learning difficulties per se.

'Adequate parenting is not a simple function of intelligence, neither is there a simple relationship between parental competence and child outcome' (p. 466). However, experience from practice suggests that in cases of serious neglect, parents with, or at the margins of, learning disability may be disproportionately represented. What is needed is a more detailed analysis of the ways in which intellectual limitations may affect parental capacity to raise their children. At present, there is not a constructive dialogue between those who identify themselves with the rights of disabled adults and those whose role is focused on the protection of children. Indeed, in some child protection cases (which I have seen in the course of my work), there can be a kind of anxious paralysis, especially in cases of neglect.

A combination of human rights ideals and sympathy for such parents, associated with uncertainty as to how much change and development is possible, can lead, on occasion, to situations manifestly harmful to the children continuing for too long. The decision to divide adult social care services from children's services tends to reinforce unhelpful identification with either the adults or their children, on both an organisational and an individual level; this is mirrored in the health and psychiatric services.

If we are to find a sensible way forward, one question has to be addressed. Is the fact of learning disability seriously relevant to an understanding of parenting deficits or is it an unwarrantable diversion from the many other interacting factors in cases of neglect? That is to say, should it be a focus for research and professional intervention? There are two ways of considering this. First, it can be viewed as an additional and contributing factor to difficulties in parenting and thus may be one more element in a downward spiral. In general, higher intelligence might make it easier to solve certain problems; bringing up children in modern society requires a range of skills, by no means all of which, as McGaw and Sturmey (1994) point out, are tied simply to parent–child interaction but require 'parent life skills' (p. 39) such as obtaining resources, both social and material. The more intelligent person (other things being equal) is likely to find this easier. Thus, it is perverse to deny or minimise the significance of this particular characteristic.

However, and second, the existence of a learning disability may of itself cause certain specific problems in child rearing. This is the area which is more controversial, yet, even when due caution about the attribution of difficulties to learning disabilities is exercised, there remain important issues about the effects of cognitive limitation on parent–child care, interaction and supervision. It seems important to give more sophisticated attention to this. To regard people with learning disabilities as in any way a heterogeneous group, about whom generalisations can be made, is plainly ridiculous, not least when one is aware of the wide range of reasons for, and the type of, such conditions. It is, however, possible to think in terms of the 'ordinary' requirements for 'good enough' parenting skills and assess the extent to which the deficits in some parents can usefully be seen in terms of cognitive difficulties. It should go without saying that other components of assessment which are customarily investigated should be the same for parents with learning disabilities as anyone else. The work of McGaw (see, for example, McGaw & Sturmey, 1994) has been influential and helpful in this. She has developed the notion of a 'parental skills model', based on 'life skills', family history, available support and resources, which takes into account for such parents many of the factors common to all similar assessments. However, we shall need to be clearer about the possible significant elements in cognitive limitation in relation to neglect.

If we consider the key factors associated with neglect, it is important to consider the parents' capacity to anticipate risk. This is crucial in the child's early years. In addition, there is the adequacy of comprehension, which includes, for example, understanding of sequences or memory for information. In discussions with practitioners, they frequently mention three areas of difficulty. One is 'not foreseeing trouble': the 'one step ahead' of ordinary parents, by which they protect the children, seems not to operate well. A second is an inability to manage situations which are diverse and complex, most particularly when a number of children simultaneously require attention. A third difficulty is of a rigidity in thought processes which makes adaptation to changed needs or situations problematic. Practitioners would do a great service to the parents and their children if these and other observations were gathered together and their implications for family support and planning for children were systematically explored. As with everyone else, these issues are bound up with issues of personality, for example of assertiveness or anxiety levels, and of characteristic modes of dealing with anger. These are not unique to people with learning disabilities but may have particular salience in certain cases.

Thus, if we are to make progress in establishing better understanding between the two sides of this debate, there are two prerequisites. First, it is essential that the workers who focus on child protection seek to distinguish those aspects of learning disability which may impede good parenting. They must be rigorous in avoiding general stigmatising assumptions and in clarifying the precise nature of the concerns. It follows that there may be a need for expert, specialised assessment, which is not only the prerogative of particular professionals, such as psychologists. For example, social workers with post-qualifying qualifications and experience in the field of child protection and learning disability are very well suited to undertaking this work.

The second prerequisite is for a greater degree of objectivity than has been evident in some of the academic discourse and an acceptance that there are some parents who have a combination of problems which makes it impossible for them to provide adequate care.

The implications of this discussion raise a number of very difficult issues. First, the judicial processes and work leading up to them needs thorough re-examination, as McConnell and Llewellyn (2002) demonstrate. Second, as has been cogently pointed out by the critics referred to earlier, even if the goodwill and wish to support that family is there, there is evidence that, too often, such parents have not received the support they need and to which they are entitled. The fact that many of those considered to have mild learning disability have not received support from adult services is compounded by similar failures in children's services. Furthermore, such parents may lack the range of informal support networks which are critical to the family's survival. Llewellyn and McConnell (2002) argue that 'mothers with learning difficulties [sic] are thought to be amongst the most socially isolated parents in the community' (p. 17). 'Generally speaking, there are family members in their lives but they remain isolated from their local communities because of the absence of friends and neighbours' (p. 29). Whether or not they are more disadvantaged in respect of other seriously neglectful families is unclear, but clearly this increases vulnerability and risk. However, there has to be a limit to the support offered to keep children safe if the day-to-day life of the family makes this unrealistic. Bluntly, if there is need for constant surveillance, advice and support, there comes a point when, short of residential care for the whole family, other plans must be made.

Third, parents with learning disabilities feature in the group of cases we have seen in many Serious Case Reviews when the very concern for the feelings of parents has led to protracted and damaging delay in taking steps to remove the children. When workers believe in the sincerity of parental intentions to love and cherish their children, it can be a heart-wrenching business.

Fourth, the parameters of the concept of neglect need to be kept in mind in relation to issues of parental competence and cognitive limitation. Of course, a range of supports may be employed to complement deficits, for example the needs of infants and young children for cognitive stimulation may be met by others, whether by relatives or projects such as Sure Start. But in the serious cases we are considering, and as the child grows older, the capacity of parents to protect their children from outside dangers, whether they be environmental hazards or sexual predators who may invade the family, are very real problems.

In summary: it is a disappointment that the two sides in this debate do not appear to have been brought closer together during the ten years since the first edition of this book. In many ways, this seems to epitomise the tension at the heart of child welfare – the rights and needs of the parents vis-à-vis the rights and needs of the children. This particular issue is, however, crying out for better information on prevalence, greater precision in the argument, better evidence for 'what works' and clearer evaluation of outcomes.

Physical health of parents

In concluding this chapter on the issues which most perplex workers with families where children are seriously neglected, I turn to the question of the physical health of parents, realistically especially mothers, about which there has been very little written. This obviously impacts on their capacity to act as effective caregivers and caretakers of their children.

Physical health cannot, in fact, be separated from other dimensions. Blackburn (1991) offers a helpful way of connecting poverty and health, in terms of the processes 'by which poverty may influence a person's susceptibility to a disease or condition' (p. 44). She suggests that there are three intertwined processes – physiological, psychological and behavioural. On the first of these, she cites much evidence to show the direct connections between poor diet and ill health, and poor housing conditions and ill health. Less familiar than the work on diet is the research on housing conditions. For example, Blackburn cites Platt *et al.* (1989), whose research on damp, cold and mould in housing conditions showed increased ill health, such as allergic reactions and respiratory infections. Although the most serious effects of this are found in children, the impact on adults should also be considered. This study also shows that physical symptoms in turn affect emotional behaviours, classically in parents described as having 'bad nerves'.

Blackburn discusses the second of these processes, psychological, in terms of the way poverty brings with it relative powerlessness and lack of control over events: 'the daily experience of poverty does little to foster a sense of being in control' (p. 45). She cites experiences of the social security system which reinforce feelings of powerlessness, but could well be applied to the health care system, in particular primary health care, so that the problem, as it were, doubles back on itself – physical health problems are not addressed, or, to combat stress, habits such as heavy smoking are adopted, which in themselves damage health.

This leads onto the third, behavioural, dimension. In the complex situations in which poor parents find themselves they may 'have to make health choices that serve to protect one aspect of health or the health of another family member whilst undermining another aspect of health or the health of another person'. These are often classed as reckless choices but 'appear to act as a mechanism for coping with some of the stresses and hardships of poverty' (p. 46). (The examples given include smoking and bottle feeding of babies.)

This discussion, of course, is relevant to many more families than those with whom this book is concerned. It reminds us of the complex but substantial evidence concerning the impact of poverty upon health and the extent of inequalities in health in modern society (Townsend *et al.*, 1988). But hard as it bears on many families, it has a particular impact on those who, for a variety of reasons discussed in this chapter, are not well equipped to do battle in an unjust society, especially those whose grip on parenting skills is precarious. It is noticeable in the extensive literature on neglect which has been reviewed here, how few comments there are about physical health and the causes and conse-quences of physical illness in parents. It would be most valuable if studies in this field were to be conducted, perhaps especially in relation to women's gynaecological well-being. Meanwhile, the professionals, especially social workers, would do a valuable service in ensuring that the question of women's physical health is systematically addressed by those competent to do so when other aspects of family functioning are being assessed.

It would be reassuring to suppose that some of this discussion in the 1980s and 1990s has been rendered redundant by the improvements in public and personal health provision and in the environment. However, the study by Ghate and Hazel in 2002, discussed in Chapter 2, is not reassuring. Although it does not focus on physical health specifically, the findings do not suggest that the earlier commentary is redundant. In any case, even if there are fewer people whose general physical health is seriously affecting their capacity to perform adequately as parents, I believe that a disproportionate number of these will be found in the families we are considering here. Rarely are these matters raised in Serious Case Reviews. Attention is focused, understandably, on the children. Yet the chronic 'poorliness' of many such mothers could be addressed. I recall a young mother who came to a residential centre and whose teeth (and those of her three-year-old) were black and rotten and whose terror of the dentist had prevented her from seeking help. The work at the centre included dealing with this as a priority.

Conclusion

Parents who seriously neglect their children share with other parents many of the same problems. This chapter, however, has sought to identify particular areas of difficulty which practitioners will recognise as recurring frequently and causing grave anxiety in terms of risk to the children. Neglect or 'omission of care' cannot be effectively addressed without an understanding of their effects upon parenting capacity.

Children Who Are Seriously Neglected

There is a huge literature on child development, much of it well evidenced. The majority of those who read this book will be familiar with the essential elements of this literature and it will not be rehearsed here in any detail. Rather, the focus is on the effects of serious neglect upon children. However, this chapter begins with a brief restatement of the foundations for healthy development. There follows a discussion of some aspects of development which are now well evidenced and which in my view merit particular emphasis at the present time. Two issues are singled out: the concept of childhood resilience and the major importance of attachment theory in understanding the impact of neglect. The chapter concludes with two matters which arise in practice when seeking to apply knowledge: the long-standing difficulties which social workers have had in working effectively with children and, more recently, the effects of government guidance on assessment on forming, and acting on, judgements concerning children's well-being in neglectful families.

The foundation for healthy development

Cooper's (1985) outline of the basic needs of children has stood the test of time very well. It was used in the guide to comprehensive assessment (DoH, 1988, the 'Orange Book') and subsequent publications from this source (e.g. DoH, 2000a; b; c) have not improved upon its clarity and direct, sensitive observation. Her guide is as follows:

- 'Basic physical care: which includes warmth, shelter, adequate food and rest, grooming (hygiene) and protection from danger.
- Affection: which includes physical contact, holding, stroking, cuddling and kissing, comforting, admiration, delight, tenderness, patience, time, making allowances for annoying behaviour, general companionship and approval.
- Security: which involves continuity of care, the expectation of continuing in the stable family unit, a predictable environment, consistent patterns of care and daily routine, simple rules and consistent controls and a harmonious family group.
- Stimulation and innate potential: by praise, by encouraging curiosity and exploratory behaviour, by developing skills through responsiveness to questions and to play, by promoting educational opportunities.
- Guidance and control: to teach adequate social behaviour which includes discipline within the child's understanding and capacity and which requires patience and a model for the child to copy, for example in honesty and concern and kindness for others.
- Responsibility: for small things at first such as self-care, tidying playthings, or taking dishes to the kitchen, and gradually elaborating the decision-making that the child has to learn in order to function adequately, gaining experience through his/her mistakes as well as his/her successes, and receiving praise and encouragement to strive and do better.
- Independence: to make his/her own decisions, first about small things but increasingly about the various aspects of his/her life within the confines of the family and society's codes. Parents use fine judgement in encouraging independence, and in letting the child see and feel the outcome of his/her own poor judgement and mistakes, but within the compass of his/her capacity. Protection is needed, but over-protection is as bad as too early responsibility and independence.' (Cooper, 1985, p. 31)

It will be readily apparent that each one of these is highly relevant to neglected children; as Cooper points out, these needs are met intuitively by 'good enough parents' and they apply to all cultures. Thus, before we begin to elaborate, refine or attempt any kind of measurement, we can do much by simply, but systematically, addressing these issues.

The effects of serious and chronic neglect

The evidence on the adverse effects of chronic neglect cited in the first edition of the book has not been challenged in subsequent years. Rather, it has been strengthened in various ways. It is therefore a matter for grave concern that the numbers of children assessed as being in danger of 'significant harm' from neglect (as indicated by their presence on the 'at risk' register) continued to rise and in recent years in the UK has settled as the highest category of child maltreatment. Furthermore, there is plenty of evidence on this issue from international sources (for example, Garbarino & Collins, 1999). One of the most authoritative in recent years is to be found in the volume edited by Dubowitz (1999), which brings together a good many of the key issues in child neglect. In the preface, Dubowitz comments that, although child abuse generally has:

> 'Evolved an intense response from the media . . . neglect has attracted far less attention . . . At the same time, it has been clear that neglect is distressingly prevalent and that the effect on children can be immense. The importance of child neglect as a major clinical and social issue is not in question'. (Dubowitz, 1999, p. vii)

There are, of course, continuing debates and uncertainties, especially concerning the longer-term effects of childhood neglect on socio-emotional functioning, including delinquency (Gaudin in Dubowitz, 1999). However, Gaudin's earlier work (1993), which reviewed this research, has not been overtaken. He concluded that 'child neglect can have devastating effects on the intellectual, physical, social and psychological development of children'.

The Bridge Consultancy (1995) report on Paul sets out a list of indicators which form a background to the detailed discussion which follows:

> 'Babies and children who are physically and emotionally neglected are at high risk of suffering:

- Gross under stimulation.
- Failure to thrive, which can lead to poor growth, developmental delay and, in an extreme form, death.
- Disturbances in emotional attachment.
- Language delay.
- Conduct disorder.
- Poor educational performance.
- Severe nappy rash and other skin infections.
- Recurrent and persistent minor infections.

As they grow older they will feel:

- Unloved and unloving.
- Powerless and hopeless.
- A severe lack of self-esteem.

- Isolated from peers and adults.' (The Bridge Consultancy, 1995, p. 3)

Pioneering work differentiating neglect from other forms of abuse was undertaken by Egeland *et al.* These two studies (1981; 1983) distinguished four patterns of maltreatment: physically abusive, hostile/verbally abusive, psychologically unavailable and neglectful. These patterns were used to investigate developmental outcomes. In the first study, a striking finding was that there was a pattern of declining function of maltreated children, especially in the 'psychologically unavailable' group. These difficulties had become apparent by 12 months and were clear by 18 months. Of those classed as 'neglected', a 'significantly higher proportion of neglected children were 'anxiously attached', at 12 and 18 months, than the control group.

These findings were used as a basis for the second study of pre-school children up to four and five years. They found that, in general, all four maltreatment groups 'continued to function poorly and were well below their age mates from similar backgrounds but who did not have a history of abuse' (p. 468). 'However, there were considerable differences between the four groups. Physically abused children were the most distractible and non-compliant' (p. 468). But it is the findings of the 'psychologically unavailable' and neglected groups which were the most striking. Most disturbingly, the former children exhibited 'a large number of pathological behaviours'. These include: 'unusual sexual behaviours; wetting or soiling, excessive appetite, repetitive movements such as rocking and self-punishing behaviours' (p. 465). The overall picture was a sorry one. The neglected children:

'Appeared to have difficulty in pulling themselves together to deal with tasks . . . They were the least flexible and creative in attempts to solve (a particular) task. Children in the neglect without physical abuse group received the lowest ratings in both self-esteem and agency (i.e. appropriate confidence and assertiveness). These same children were also the most dependent and demonstrated the lowest ego control in the preschool.' (Egeland *et al.*, 1983, p. 469)

No subsequent research (for example Crouch & Milner, 1993; Ney *et al.*, 1994) has findings which challenge the general thrust of this work. Rather, studies have elaborated and developed this gloomy picture. The early studies by Egeland *et al.* (1988a; b) took into account the interaction of some different types of maltreatment which can obviously coexist. Thus, physical abuse, with or without neglect and vice versa, were also measured. It appears, however, that the possibility of combined 'psychological unavailability and neglect' was not taken into account in their studies and that neglect was defined more narrowly, in terms of 'irresponsible and incompetent managing of child care activities' (p. 462), than we are here considering. Thus, in reporting the findings, I have assumed the category of 'psychological unavailability' of mothers is likely to be in some cases a part of a neglectful pattern. The combination of the two strengthens the possibility of powerfully adverse consequences for the child.

Most of the research which has been reviewed above concerns the extensive and far-reaching consequences of neglect upon the children's social and emotional development. However, concentration upon these subtle and complex matters should not lead us to minimise the serious effects of physical neglect per se. Cooper's (1985) outline of the needs of children puts basic physical care at the top of the list but passes over it briefly: 'warmth, shelter, adequate food and rest, grooming (hygiene), and protection from danger'. Perhaps she thought 'it is so obvious'. Indeed, yet how is it that a stage can be reached when, by any standards, a child or children are not receiving sufficient care to meet these basic needs and yet action has not been taken? The case of Paul (The Bridge Consultancy, 1995) starkly reminds us of the tragic consequences of physical neglect. Paul, aged 18 months:

> 'Had lain in urine soaked bedding and clothes for a considerable number of days. [He had] burns over most of his body derived from the urine staining, plus septicaemia with septic lesions at the ends of his fingers and toes. In addition, he was suffering from severe pneumonia.' (The Bridge Consultancy, 1995, p. 7)

More recently, a report commissioned by Sheffield Area Child Protection Committee on 'the W family' (Cantrill, 2005) charted a case of the gravest neglect, which was brought to a sad conclusion by the admission to hospital of two of the five children, twins of 13 months, both critically ill. One of the twins weighed only 4.1 kg and required full resuscitation and ventilation. The other twin required urgent intravenous resuscitation.

Such cases are thankfully rare and inquiries afterwards demonstrate that complex interacting factors, both in family behaviour and interagency cooperation, all play a part in the ultimate tragedy. However, in the context of this discussion, the lesson, over and over again, is the need to focus attention on the detail of the care being offered and to be aware that, in cases of neglect, we may be on a slippery slope, in which 'more or less' good enough parenting slips to 'not good enough' and thence to 'quite inadequate'. It is this 'slippery slope' which has posed so many difficulties in taking decisions and to professional relief when there is an 'incident'. There are basic norms of development to guide professionals, such as the percentile charts, and it is indefensible for these not to be utilised. The Bridge Consultancy report notes that some of the older children in Paul's family had been described from babyhood onwards as 'grossly overweight . . . Such a condition can be as much an indicator of neglect as where a child fails to thrive' (p. 173).

In the end, judgements as to whether physical care is 'good enough' must be taken on the basis of an assessment of its various components by the agencies and professionals qualified to do so. Whilst there may be some difficult questions concerning differing cultural or class standards by which these matters should be judged (Chapter 3), these can be overstated in matters of basic physical care. Indeed, one suspects that such debates can serve as a diversion from the more important questions as to why serious physical neglect has been so difficult to address satisfactorily.

It is pertinent also to consider the place of food and feeding within the context of physical care, as well as its deep emotional significance. There are examples of children who, quite simply, do not get enough food of any kind and are hungry. The reasons for this, however, are very varied. There may be problems of managing on a low income; as indicated in Chapter 2, there are many families living (or trying to live) on an income well below the official poverty line. Such problems, linked sometimes to lack of understanding of nutritional needs, should always be the first point of exploration. However, this by itself is not sufficient to understand the reasons underlying nutritional difficulties. The extensive research (Skuse, 1985) conducted concerning non-organic 'failure to thrive' indicates that such children do indeed fail to get enough calories to sustain development. But the patterns of interaction which can be observed between parents and their young children suggest a wide range of behaviours leading to the problem. It is important that we include neglected children and their mothers in such observations, rather than putting them in a class apart, bearing in mind that attitudes to food, feeding and being fed are bound up with past and recent, good and bad experiences. It is also basic to our understanding of the situation that a hungry child is an anxious child, and that experiences of hunger carried forward have profound effects on subsequent behaviour through childhood to adult life. What is it like to be hungry, day after day, week after week, month after month?

Infants and young children

There are some critical issues concerning physical health of infants and young children which we have become more aware of in recent years. One of these concerns the health of infants born to parents who abuse drugs or alcohol. This should be put in the wider context of the 'conditions needed for the optimal development of the child' (Cleaver *et al.*,

1999, p. 48). Cleaver *et al.* point out that the well-being of the unborn child requires that the mother has an adequate diet, should not smoke heavily and should avoid certain medications. This is well known and familiar to professionals. It is important that those who work with seriously neglectful parents recognise how adverse the effects on the baby of maternal lifestyle can be, even before the effects of substance abuse are considered. Cleaver *et al.* confirm that 'there is little dispute that excessive parental drinking or drug use negatively affects the unborn child' (p. 49). However, 'what is in dispute is the degree and nature of the impact' (p. 49). What is established includes evidence that cocaine and heroin are 'particularly damaging because they may cause placental detachment, stillbirth, premature birth, lower birth weight and microcephaly' (p. 49). There is also the possibility that the baby may be born addicted. A further possible consequence of intravenous drug use is that the unborn child contracts HIV or hepatitis C. Excessive use of alcohol by a mother in pregnancy can cause foetal alcohol syndrome, which may damage the central nervous system. Interestingly, Cleaver *et al.* also refer to evidence that fathers who are heavy drinkers may produce children with lower birth weight and increased risk of heart defects (p. 50).

Cleaver *et al.*, and the sources upon which the authors draw, demonstrate conclusively that parents who are caught up in various forms of 'body abuse' place the foetus at risk. There is some uncertainty about the nature of the causal links and the effects of various drugs (such as ecstasy). Good early antenatal care can ameliorate the effects to some extent and it is by no means inevitable that the babies will be damaged before birth or suffer long-term effects. However, it is essential that workers involved face the possibility of this early harm and include these considerations in their assessment and planning for the well-being of such children.

The cognitive development of neglected children is another issue which has come to the forefront in recent years. We are much clearer now about the significance of early relationships in this process. Technical and theoretical advances have enabled a better understanding about the ways in which the structure and growth of our brains in infancy and early childhood is affected by early experiences. One of the most authoritative summaries of the present state of knowledge is to be found in the US National Clearinghouse on Child Neglect and Abuse information review (2001). In their introduction, quoting Shore (1997), they point out that:

'It appears that genetics predispose us to develop in certain ways. But our interactions with our environment have a significant impact on how our predispositions will be expressed; these interactions organise our brain's development and, therefore, shape the person we become'. (National Clearinghouse on Child Neglect and Abuse, 2001)

This review includes references to lack of stimulation as an aspect of neglect:

> 'A failure to meet a child's cognitive, emotional or social needs . . . For a child to master developmental tasks in these areas, they need opportunities, encouragement and acknowledgement from their caregivers. If this stimulation is lacking during children's early years, the weak neuronal pathways that had been developed in expectation of these experiences may wither and die – the children may not achieve the usual developmental milestones'. (National Clearinghouse on Child Neglect and Abuse, 2001, p. 7)

[handwritten margin note: Child development]

This important summary of the cognitive damage to children from severe neglect is of crucial importance in formulating policies for intervention in neglectful families. The stimulation to which it refers is part of the everyday knowledge and experience of ordinary families; the verbal interaction, the shared babble, 'the face-to-face baby talk and . . . endless repetition of sounds . . . builds the brain circuitry, which will enable the child eventually to say words and form sentences' (p. 7). How often do workers with neglectful families note 'language delay' in toddlers, a problem which is the basis of continuing educational problems?

[handwritten margin note: Speech therapy]

Davies (2002) makes helpful links between infant brain research and the neurobiological effects of trauma and neglect and the 'experience–dependent nature of brain development in infancy'. She focuses on 'certain windows of time' which are critical for the creation of the brain pathways which lead, *inter alia*, to 'attention, perception . . . and language' (p. 422).

The National Clearinghouse review refers to 'global neglect' in relation to the multiple deprivation of language, touch and social contact experienced by children in some 'orphanages' or institutions for infants and young children (p. 9). A graphic scan is shown of markedly different brain sizes in a normal and seriously neglected child of three years (Perry, 1996). Although evidence is now more sophisticated and detailed, the tragic effects of such severe deprivation have been long known, even although the precise physiological effects were not. I recall learning about it when I was a student. Rutter *et al.* (1999) point out that the early studies of this type of deprivation overstated 'both the frequency of this outcome and its inevitability' (p. 537). However, the impact of these early theories on social work was significant for it contributed to a recognition of the damaging effects of impersonal institutional care on young children, with consequent changes in placement policy. More emphasis was at that time placed on the adverse emotional consequences, whereas recent research has enabled us to connect this with the cognitive consequences of the same experiences of 'global' neglect. This is entirely consistent with the holistic model for the understanding of neglect on development.

However, there has been very little attempt to connect that literature on 'global neglect' and institutional care with the growing concern about the position of young children growing up in seriously neglectful families. Thankfully, it is, of course, very unlikely that the conditions prevailing in the notorious 'orphanages' would be replicated within a family. Nonetheless, the additional evidence now available on the development of infant and young children's brains should remind us of the potential for significant and enduring harm when the normal processes of stimulation within a relationship are missing or seriously deficient. This aspect of the early years should be a key element in the assessment of well-being.

School-age children and young people

The critical importance of early years for subsequent development does not mean that the later effects of neglect can be minimised; indeed, current assessment must include an attempt to understand what has been positive or negative in the early years and its likely effect on present behaviour and attitudes. Building on good experiences may be part of working to support resilience, which is discussed later.

Experienced practitioners are well used to seeing physical health problems in older neglected children; sometimes these have their roots in the unpromising start to their lives, but they may be reinforced by the current neglectful behaviour of parents or caretakers. There is frequently inattention to children's medical needs. Some child protection procedures refer to this specifically as an element of neglect. There are many examples, both in published reports or inquiries and in internal reviews following child deaths, of a pattern of missed health appointments. Not all of these relate to serious medical conditions, but neglect of children with minor physical problems, such as those connected with hearing and sight, can further reinforce the disadvantage and stigma, particularly at school, from which so many neglected children already suffer. A squint, for example, can prompt mockery and teasing from other children. Whilst caution must be exercised in the weight and significance which is placed on 'missed appointments', taken in conjunction with other elements in neglect, or standing out in their frequency, it is clear that the cumulative impact on the health of children necessitates careful attention.

As we have seen, the early years are critical in relation to cognitive, as well as emotional, developments. This is carried forward into the school years and has major implications for subsequent intellectual and emotional attainment. Many seriously neglected children start school (or even nursery school) well behind their peers. At this time, we have a continuing debate and disagreement in the UK about the education of children with 'special needs'. How children are officially categorised as having special needs is outside the scope of this discussion. There is, however, no doubt that the children here considered will usually have special educational needs. If they are to overcome initial disadvantage, they will require skilled attention, recognising that emotional and intellectual needs are inseparable for effective learning.

A further issue to consider relates to standards of educational attainment. At a time in the UK when the special needs of children may be inadequately served by a competitive ethos in schools and by resource constraints, it is particularly disturbing that studies have shown neglected children to be the most seriously affected educationally of maltreated children. Kurtz *et al.* (1993a) commented that 'there is a pressing need for well contrived studies that examine the developmental consequences of abuse and neglect on the school-aged children' (p. 581). Their study concluded: 'academic failure emerged as the single and most consistent risk factor for neglected children' (p. 587). Furthermore, 'the neglect group's rate of absences for the year prior to implementation of the study was nearly five times that of the comparison group' (p. 587). As these authors, and others, point out, this should not surprise us:

> 'Intellectual development depends heavily on the ongoing quality of parent child interaction . . . Low educational aspirations, lack of encouragement for learning, a lack of language stimulation, non-participation in school activities and unresponsiveness to the child's achievement all undermine school success.' (Kurtz *et al.*, 1993a, p. 588)

A particular facet of this, to which reference is made in various studies, relates to language development, clearly the key to educational attainment (Allen & Oliver, 1982; Fox & Dingwall, 1988). The lack of stimulation in early years which is so characteristic of such families means that the amazing linguistic achievements of this period in normal children are 'dulled'. Small wonder that such children are later found to be 'at extreme risk of school failure' (Kurtz *et al.*, 1993b, p. 100).

Reviews of the evidence on these matters, such as that by Crouch and Milner (1993), rightly draw attention to the limitations of some studies, for example in terms of sample size or bias, and to confusions regarding the definitions of 'neglect' used. But there is a feeling of anger and sadness that the cumulative impact of these studies, when set beside what is known about the necessary conditions for optimal development, has not been more effectively utilised by child welfare services. Put at its crudest, we heap up trouble for the future. As Ney *et al.* (1994) movingly put it:

> 'Our evidence supports the hypothesis that the most severe psychological conflicts arise from neglect. Having been deprived of the necessary ingredients in their normal development, children never seem to accept the loss of a childhood that could have been. They keep searching as adolescents and adults, only to find those they search amongst are usually themselves deprived people who not only cannot provide them with what they needed as children, but also tend to abuse them, partly out of their own frustrations in encountering somebody who they thought would give to them when they are so hungry.' (Ney *et al.*, 1994, p. 711)

Everyone who works with such families will recognise that description. It may well be that the persisting difficulties which looked-after children have in achieving satisfactory educational standards have their roots in the failure to grasp the nettle in the early years of school life. The excellent objectives of Sure Start and similar initiatives may require reappraisal in relation to this small group of chronically deprived children.

The school years are a time in which a child's experience and knowledge is hugely widened. He or she is put in touch with people outside the family who are important and influential. Relationships with peers as well as adults are a source of joy and pain. As we shall later discuss, working with the social networks which are potentially available to provide alternative supports and sources of fulfilment may be a crucial part of 'complementary care'. This is, however, a delicate and difficult business, for there may be much in the behaviour and attitudes of such children (and their families) which is 'a turn off' to others. In considering the ingredients of serious neglect, there has been a tendency to concentrate on its most tangible features – dirty, ill-clothed children for example. These, of course, make an impact on those outside the family; schoolteachers, for example, know all too well the reactions of their students to the smelly newcomer. A key aspect of parental neglect, inadequate supervision, is not only about placing children at physical risk or at risk of stigma. It also means that the children are inadequately socialised. They do not learn the rules of the society in which they find themselves. They pay a high price for this deviance, part of which is described as 'social exclusion'.

Delinquency and antisocial behaviour

A number of the children from neglectful families are drawn into behaviour which is socially unacceptable or illegal. In Chapter 5, I will discuss the problems which arise in 'working together' because of the fragmentation of the systems of 'welfare' and 'justice'. Here, my focus is upon the children and young people themselves and upon societal responses to them. Seriously neglected children form only a small part of the population described as 'delinquent and antisocial'. It is evident that our society is in the throes of one of the recurring crises about its young people; there are major questions about the social climate and culture which cannot be explored here. However, it is reasonable to suppose that the situation of the children who are the focus of this book is adversely affected by the wider manifestations of the tensions between the generations.

Parental failure (for whatever reason) to control and supervise children is part of the pattern of serious neglect. Badly behaved young people are currently high profile in the media. This brings in its train political responses intended to reassure the general public. We are all familiar with the mantra 'tough on crime and tough on the causes of crime' but to operationalise this has proved exceedingly difficult. The plethora of 'Antisocial Behaviour Orders' and the high number which are breached illustrate this quite neatly.

The problem which confronts us in this book is profound. Many neglected children have not been offered adequate models, in the context of loving relationships, upon which to base their own behaviour. Some of these children simply do not learn how to behave in ways of which the wider society approves. As they grow older, they become aware that they are not 'acceptable' to many of their peers and the adults around them but they lack the insight and social skills to change. They may seek companionship with others who have similar or related difficulties, which compounds the problem.

What has occurred is what may be described as a 'double whammy'. These children have not developed normal attachments to their primary carers; thus, they do not have the inner security which is derived from those early stable relationships. Their behaviour is often designed to attract attention, one way or another. But it often takes the form of antisocial or delinquent behaviour, which evolves punitive responses. Before they can change, they need emotional evidence that someone cares about them as individuals and will combine nurture with control. At the core of the problem which these children present is 'privation', that is, they have lacked the essentials for healthy development. 'Deprivation' implies something has been taken away. This is a correct description for the experiences of some children; admittedly, it is, to some extent, a matter of degree rather than an absolute distinction. But, just as some children in 'orphanages' can only be described as suffering from privation, so it is for some of the children here considered.

Logic and evidence, not sentimentality, dictate that punishment, without any concurrent complementary, healing relationships is doomed to failure. These relationships may occur spontaneously without official intervention, as when a new adult enters a child's life and offers a fresh start. However, the characteristic behaviour of the antisocial child or young person makes it likely that such critical relationships will need supporting and facilitating.

Such observations may sound unrealistic. However, we have already seen modest, but very exciting, initiatives, such as the project televised in Birmingham showing a group of 'troublesome' young people achieving a high standard of discipline and control in a ballet performance, (*Ballet Hoo*, 2004, Channel 4) with huge enjoyment. The key factor in such projects is that support, warmth and encouragement to individuals by individuals is offered, within a demanding framework for personal responsibility.

In 'Working Together' (Chapter 5), this topic will be discussed in relation to the problems raised by the fragmentation of our justice and welfare systems.

The concept of resilience

The idea of childhood 'resilience' as offering some protection in the face of adversity is well established and welcome in a field which has revealed so starkly the damage which may be done to children who are maltreated. It is not surprising that it has been espoused with enthusiasm by some of those who contribute to the child welfare literature. (See, for example, Daniel *et al.*, 1999.) It is self-evidently true that some children seem to survive and even to prosper in families in which the dice seem loaded against them; furthermore, their adult lives show that this capacity to cope with life is sustained. Whether we attribute 'resilience' to basic genetic endowments or to successful elements in early relationships, or both, there is no doubt that some rise above adversity, including a neglectful upbringing. The key question for practitioners is whether and in what ways this essential quality can be harnessed and developed. In the files of neglectful families held by social services departments, there is often a lack of differentiation in the descriptions of children. Their parents, in contrast to 'ordinary' ones, may themselves find it difficult to pinpoint the special traits of their children. The children may play a part in this, if their behaviour lacks the distinctiveness and sparkle which characterises most children. Part of the importance of a carefully individualised assessment of each child in a family is to ensure that strengths and 'copability' are pinpointed. Behind the chaos or the depression in the household, there are children with distinct characteristics. The extent of their resilience, as of their vulnerability, needs to be appraised. Daniel *et al.*, (1999) explore these issues at length. They utilise the definition of resilience given by Fonagy *et al.* (1994) as 'normal development under difficult conditions'. A substantial part of their analysis deals with the factors which can build on, and consolidate, what may be regarded as 'potential for resilience'. However, their focus is not on neglect per se but on aspects of maltreatment more generally.

Unfortunately, we see children in neglectful families who seem to have few of the early benign experiences which lay the basis for resilience; when we see them coping well, we may have to fall back on the vaguer (although very important) indications of genetic endowment which strengthens them. However, we do well to explore some of the less obvious aspects of their early lives which may explain their coping capacity. Werner (1990) and Daniel *et al.* (1999) suggest some of these factors. Werner points out that 'resilient infants tend to have predictable temperamental characteristics which elicit positive responses for other people' (p. 100). Neglectful parents who vacillate in their responses may be more forthcoming with a responsive child, especially when parents are ambivalent about parenting (see Chapter 3). There are other resilience factors within the family. The child has a better chance if a close bond has been established with at least one person in the first year of life. This finding underlines the importance of taking a detailed family history. Second, close ties with alternative caregivers, even outside the family, may be of great significance. Third, and much less discussed, is the relationship with siblings; this can be either as caregiver or as the recipient and can be a major preventative factor for vulnerable children (p. 66). There are crucial questions concerning the positive and negative aspects of sibling relationships which require detailed exploration (Dunn & Plomin, 1990) in relation to the decision as to whether children remain at home or are removed.

Daniel *et al.* (1999) also explore the wide variety of other experiences outside the family which can reinforce coping capacities in the child. The essential focus for intervention to support resilience will be to find people and activities which will help build self-confidence and self-esteem and, crucially, will encourage 'a belief in . . . self-efficacy and ability to deal with change and adaption' (p. 68). Although relationships are often integral to these developments, interests in particular activities and success in pursuing them, especially in adolescence, can be a way forward for a young person whose capacity for constructive attachment has been damaged and for whom there needs to be an escape route from emotional turmoil.

Attachment

There is now available a significant body of research and theory on the nature of attachment between young children and their primary care-givers which has assumed major significance in the study of child development. In the years 1956–1970, since Bowlby brought together psychoanalytic insights and the evidence from animal studies, a sophisticated body of evidence has been built up which builds on his early work. It is indispensable for social workers and other professionals working in the field of child welfare and child protection, and cannot be explored here at the length it deserves. Current texts which are likely to prove invaluable for students and workers are Howe (2005) and Prior and Glaser (2006). Both draw extensively on the work of Crittenden, one aspect of whose work (a typology of neglectful parents) has already been described in Chapter 3 (Crittenden, 1999).

The main focus of this discussion will be on the effects of seriously neglectful parents on the essential processes of early attachment and its likely effects on subsequent development. But it is important first to grasp the essential elements of the concept. This is particularly well articulated by Prior and Glaser (2006). Amongst the essential points they make are:

- 'Attachment theory has a specific meaning, both in terms of its nature and the person to whom it implies' (p. 15). That is to say, it is not an alternative word for affection, devotion or love.
- 'Attachment behaviour is proximity seeking to the attachment figure in the face of threat' (p. 16).
- 'The level of activation [of attachment behaviour] depends on the level of the child's discomfort or their perception of the severity of the threat' (p. 18).
- In this specific context, 'an attachment is a bind or tie between an individual and an attachment figure ... Attachment is a tie based on a need for safety, security and protection. This need is paramount in infancy and childhood, when the developing child is immature and vulnerable.' It is *instinctive* and 'invariably refers to their primary carer' (p. 15).
- 'Mental representations of the infant-child and their human environment are formed on the basis of early attachment experiences ... "Internal working models" can be updated' (p. 23), in the light of later experiences.

Achieving 'good enough' attachment is crucial for subsequent satisfactory relationships, but it also lays the foundation for many other aspects of development. An infant or young child who is securely attached is free to learn; trust in their primary caregiver can be transferred to other adults; in infancy, close encounters with other adults and other children are a rich source of stimulation. Cognitive, as well as emotional, development is inextricably bound up with early attachment. The capacity of the toddler to go adventuring is dependent on feeling safe enough — the attachment figure is present or can be found without too much difficulty.

This is now widely accepted. Prior and Glaser (2006) show that various studies:

'Followed in many different cultures, all . . . found attachment theory to be applicable across cultures. What may differ across cultures is the expression of maternal sensitivity and the manifestations of secure-base behaviour. These behavioural differences do not invalidate the applicability of the theory.' (Prior & Glaser, 2006, p. 81)

Research in the past 30 years has identified distortions in the unhealthy responses of infants and children to experiences of inadequate or negative parenting. However, it is important to understand that there can be many variations in the interactions of the primary caregiver and child which would not be regarded as ideal but which do not result in irremediable damage; compensatory factors (especially other people), difficulties resolved in time and natural resilience all play a part in this. Nonetheless, it is sadly apparent that in the more serious cases of neglect, significant harm in the development of normal attachment may be evident from an early stage. These distortions are now better understood and it is essential that workers in the field use this knowledge when they are making judgements about the future of children.

Howe (2005) explores these issues in depth, drawing on the most recent evidence and research. Children who are neglected are often subject to other forms of maltreatment which complicate their responses. He also considers the impact on attachment which particular problems, such as drugs, depression and domestic violence in parents, are likely to have on children. Work with neglectful families cannot be effective without serious attention to this complex aspect of the parent–child (usually mother) relationship. Although there are many other factors to take into account in weighing up the critical question: 'do these children have a future at home with their parent(s)?' the 'attachment issue' lays the foundation for so much else.

Howe (2005) describes the three basic types of attachment as 'secure, avoidant or ambivalent' (p. 30). He suggests that these depend on the sensitivity and interest of the caregiver. We need also to recognise that the infant brings to the relationship certain basic traits which may interact positively or negatively with the caregiver. Both ambivalent and avoidant patterns may be seen when parents are seriously neglectful; neglect is often associated with other forms of maltreatment. Neglect simply describes an omission of care; it does not explain the reasons for the omissions.

Secure attachments are formed when caregiving is 'sufficiently sensitive, loving, responsive, attained, consistent, available and accepting' (Howe, 2005, p. 31). This sounds idealistic but it is in fact readily recognisable in the unself-conscious behaviour of ordinary parents everywhere. Howe (2005) relates his analysis of avoidant and ambivalent attachments to the typology proposed by Crittenden (1999) and outlined in Chapter 3 (pp. 50–53). This includes both disorganised neglect and depressed, passive and physical neglect.

Disorganised neglect

The crucial aspect of parenting which affects attachment processes lies in the preoccupation of parents with their own feelings and needs. 'They are neither sensitive nor consistently responsive to their children's needs and anxieties'. *There is no pattern to their caregiving behaviour* (p. 20). 'The child experiences the caregiver as underinvolved . . . There is little emotional attunement' (p. 120). Howe suggests that such parents may find coping with babies is easier than when children begin 'to explore and assert their autonomy' (p. 121) and paints a graphic picture of households in which 'anger and helplessness lend to much shouting and drama' (p. 123). He describes the responses of infants and toddlers to such situations in terms which will be readily recognisable to social workers and other professionals. 'They are fractious, irritable and not easily soothed. They whine, cling, fret and fuss longer than other children. By the age of three or four, these attention seeking behaviours become even more pronounced' (p. 125). 'The big worry is to be ignored and not to be involved' (p. 126). They learn that they must increase 'the volume and frequency of distress signals' (p. 127) and/or engage in seductive behaviour to keep the attention of the attachment figure.

Inevitably, such children become more difficult to control as they grow older. If a child has no faith in the settled interest and concern of the primary caregiver, he or she has to create situations with adults which may elicit the desired responses. Many people get caught up in the maelstrom, including the professionals.

Depressed, passive and physical neglect

Howe (2005) describes such families as:

'Lost in an empty world of their own. Relationships are lifeless and dull . . . In terms of basic care, only the bare minimum takes place . . . Care tends to occur when the parent remembers or becomes sufficiently energised; it does not happen in response to the child's attachment signals.' (Howe, 2005, p. 136)

Of particular concern is the lack of supervision of the children. The effect on the children is profound because 'the emotional energy has drained out of the system' (p. 137). Thus, the children become 'listless and incurious' (p. 137). They do not feel that they are making an impact on their caregivers. 'The failure to use either affect or cognition to organise information about reality closes the door to both relationships and learning' (p. 140). A young child in this situation is in urgent need of emotional food.

Earlier in this chapter, reference has been made to the evidence of the impact of neglect upon children in some institutional care. Global neglect in its most extreme form begins (but does not end) with failure to provide an attachment figure. The early formulations of Bowlby (1969; 1973) in which 'protest, despair and detachment' were seen to be the phases of such children's reactions to the absence of an attachment figure are now established in the literature of child development and of children's and adults' reactions to loss. Thankfully, social workers in the UK rarely see families in which the grossest aspects of institutional neglect are replicated and children are in the third phase of 'detachment', or utter hopelessness. (Those workers, including myself, who have seen this in institutions, will never forget it.) But there are occasionally such cases in which it appears that the basic biological need of a child to find security and stimulation with a primary caregiver has not been met. Such cases are most likely to arise in the most serious forms of parental substance abuse. Howe (2005) is at his most cogent on this point:

'As drugs and alcohol are mind altering substances, they seriously tamper with that beautiful mind-minded synchrony between parent and child that characterises sensitive, attuned, reciprocal parenting . . . Emotional availability and understanding disappear'. (Howe, 2005, p. 183)

In summary: this discussion of the impact of parental neglect upon the development of satisfactory attachment to caregivers in early childhood is a challenge to all who work professionally with such families. The evidence of its importance is overwhelming. It does not appear that this has been adequately understood by those who formulate policy and supervise practice. It has major implications for the children's futures within their families (including critical issues about the timeframe for children's development) and for the details of care plans designed to enhance parental capacity or complementary relationships before it is too late.

Social work with neglected children

Thus far, the focus has been on seriously neglected children and their needs. Many workers are involved in such families; the roles of health professionals and teachers may be pivotal in some cases. If attachment processes are grossly distorted, there may well be a need for specialist mental health intervention. However, the role of the social worker is central. Social workers are usually at the centre of assessment and care planning. To do this effectively they must understand the essentials for healthy child development, the effects of neglect in all developmental domains and be able to apply this to specific families. This includes observing children and reflecting on what they observe. This is not a detached process. It involves interaction with the children as well as the adults.

British law places the interests of the child at the centre of decision making in the child welfare services. It is somewhat ironic, therefore, that social workers are in general less comfortable in observing and communicating with children than adults. It is important to reflect upon the reasons why this might be so. In the early post-war days of professional education for 'child care officers', considerable importance was attached to the direct observation of, and rapport with, children. Residential child care placements during training were a required element in the course. In the 1950s, memories of the traumatic effects of evacuation upon wartime children were still fresh and had profoundly affected a group of experts in child development who were predominantly psychoanalytic in orientation. The names on the reading lists of all child care officer students included: Barbara Dockar Drysdale (Principal of the Mulberry Bush School for emotionally disturbed children); Anna Freud, a psychoanalyst whose work concerning young children in wartime nurseries was influential; Melanie Klein, a psychoanalyst who had pioneered the analysis of young children; Susan Isaacs, psychologist and psychoanalyst who had written weekly columns for the magazine *Nursery World*; Clare Winnicott, a psychiatric social worker, and Donald Winnicott, a paediatrician and psychoanalyst whose influence on social work was profound and who, in popular broadcasts, coined the phrase 'good enough mothering', which now has general currency.

These people were profoundly influential for a generation of social work educators. At the same time, John Bowlby's work (1969; 1973) on bonding and attachment was increasingly being recognised as crucially important to child welfare social work. This was epitomised in

films made by James and Joyce Robertson on the impact on a young child of going to hospital (Robertson & Robertson, 1953) or of entering residential care at 17 months (Robertson & Robertson, 1969). All child welfare social work students (and many others) saw these films. The grief, anxiety and despair of these young children, separated from their caregivers, left an indelible impression on all who saw them – including, it was reported, the then Secretary for State for Health and Social Services, Sir Keith Joseph. Policy for parents to stay with their children in hospital was shaped by these films. Even after these influences waned, the Tavistock Clinic was a focal point of continuing efforts to demonstrate the value of these approaches, involving close observation of children, for social workers and other professionals, and maintaining a valuable presence even when the general climate became inhospitable (Trowell & Bower, 1995). Gradually, however, the emphasis on direct observation of young children dropped away and no longer received explicit attention in the training of social workers. The emphasis on attention to detail in seeking to understand the meaning of a child's behaviour was no longer highly valued. This coincided with an 'information explosion' in the broad areas of activity in social work which posed serious strains and dilemmas for educators in the selection of material for basic training and a growing attention to child protection within that part of the curriculum rather than to child welfare more generally. Paradoxically, however, for reasons discussed below, this concentration on child protection was not accompanied by a clarification of the place of child observation within that sphere of the work. On the contrary, a number of child abuse inquiry reports commented unfavourably on the deficiencies in this sphere, notably that concerning Jasmine Beckford (Brent Borough Council, 1985). In some ways, its overheated style and harshly censorious tone concerning individuals makes one reluctant to cite it yet again. But the point made is powerful, and the analysis of the case of Paul (The Bridge Consultancy, 1995), unfortunately suggests that the lesson has still not been learnt.

> 'Throughout the three years of social work with the Beckfords, Ms Wahlstrom totally misconceived her role as the field worker enforcing Care Orders in respect of two very young children at risk. Her gaze focused on Beverley Lorrington and Morris Beckford; she averted her eyes from the children to be aware of them only as and when they were with their parents, hardly ever to observe their development, and never to communicate with Jasmine on her own. The two children were regarded as mere appendages to their parents who were treated as the clients. (In the meticulous record of nearly 100 pages of detailed notes kept by Ms Wahlstrom and others in the social worker's report there is not a single entry devoted exclusively to Jasmine and Louise.)'
> (Brent Borough Council, 1985, p. 293)

Ten years later, the report on Paul comments:

'We have already indicated that we are alarmed at the lack of entries in records which show what the children were saying or thinking about their situation. There was information, of course; perhaps there are two issues that need to be addressed. First, when information is available it needs to be taken seriously and evaluated; for example, the concerns that we have already referred to in relation to the children being dirty and smelly.' (The Bridge Consultancy, 1995)

Helping children to communicate difficulties, wishes and feelings is a skilled task which should be part of the social work and police role within the child protection process. When faced with these kinds of signals it is important to interview the children within the child protection procedures, to establish how they see life within the family. The word 'interview' has a rather formal ring to it. However, there are now very many creative ways of enabling children to express their views, their wishes and their feelings. It is possible to use art, play, drama, children's stories and computers to enable children to express their views. As far as we can judge, prior to Paul's death and excluding the incidents relating to suspected sexual abuse, attempts at obtaining the children's views were very limited:

'We cannot stress too highly how important it is, when dealing with families who are in touch with social services, that there is a clear methodology which allows for skilled, creative discussions with children and young people. They are living the experience and can give a more accurate picture of what life is like in a family than any assessment made externally by a professional.' (The Bridge Consultancy, 1995, pp. 171–2)

However, the Victoria Climbié inquiry (Laming, 2003) revealed yet again that a child, 'a person', had been left in the shadows by most of the workers in contact with her. There was no coherent or consistent attempt to observe or communicate with her. (The fact that she spoke French and no translator was used compounded the inadequacy of the management of the case.) The incompetence revealed by the inquiry must not be taken as an indication that most work in child protection was of that standard. (Certain areas of the country have had much greater difficulty in recruiting and retaining staff than others.) But it is critically important to address the question – what has led to this weakness in child care practice and why has it persisted for so long?

There would appear to be three interlocking strands. The first arises from the association of child observation and communication with psychoanalytic theory. We have earlier discussed the pervasive effects of a sociological critique of social work which accused the profession of using individualistic explanation of their clients' problems to avoid consideration of, and action on, social problems. As psychoanalytic theory and its derivatives were jettisoned, so social workers were left without working theories for use with children, who got sidelined in the wider ideological debate. Even theory such as that used in behavioural approaches, which bore no relation to psychoanalysis (Jehu *et al.*, 1972), did not find much favour in the ideological climate of the time. Such was the power of the prevailing socio-political analysis. The lack of an acceptable theoretical basis for work with children partly accounts for social workers' loss of confidence in their capacity to perform this part of the work and loss of conviction in its importance. Indeed, it may well be that an increasing trend towards the use of 'experts' in court cases reflects this insecurity.

There is, however, an exception to this 'theoretical vacuum'; this relates to 'attachment theory', already discussed. This body of theory, closely related to, but separate from, the wider fields of psychodynamic theory, was highly significant in the early days of social work education. But as 'child protection' became a specialism within child welfare work, attachment theory was much less used by child protection practitioners than in the related field of fostering and adoption. There was a continuing acceptance of its significance for a child whose experiences of family life were fragmented and disrupted, but much less understanding of the diverse ways in which 'attachment' could be dysfunctional or inadequate for the child at home with the birth family. During the period when many social workers in child protection seemed to stop noticing children, their colleagues, in long-term teams and in voluntary agencies concerned with fostering and adoption, were busy developing creative work with children, much of it derived from the very same psychoanalytic or related theory, notably that surrounding the concept of 'attachment' (see, for example, Aldgate & Simmonds, 1988). They doggedly pursued such approaches, often in an organisational and professional climate which was unsympathetic.

The weaknesses described above were less evident in the work of staff in family centres, (now to be known as children's centres). Indeed, staff from varying backgrounds in these centres, including those with nursery nurse or teacher training, had little difficulty (to put it simply) in 'noticing' children's behaviour. However, neither did many of the social workers in the same setting. It is clearly not *sui generis*. Nor can it be generally attributed to the 'youth' of social workers, a large number of whom were middle-aged parents. Not for the first time, we must look to the rather alarming impact of role expectations and reinforcement within field settings for an explanation.

It would seem that the effect of the trend towards a forensic model of child protection, which laid great stress on the investigation of 'incidents' or 'happenings', deflected workers in investigative roles away from a more holistic and integrated view of children and their developmental needs. The management of sexual abuse investigations both confuses and confirms this analysis. Intensive interviewing by police and social workers together, for 'disclosure', highlighted the difficulties in which the forensic approach has placed child protection workers. In these interviews, play materials are used and children are watched and listened to carefully. Yet these 'forensically directed' interviews have not redressed the balance. Within their own framework, concerned with legal process and evidence, the specialist police are often better trained than the social workers. Because the latter often lack any sound theoretical framework on which to base their work, this sometimes results in an imbalance of power between the two professions. Most importantly, the nature and extent of therapeutic work with children before court hearings, and the skills required to practise it, have been seriously hindered by legal requirements.

That which is lost can be found. The guidance issued by the Department of Health (2000a; b; c), a framework for assessment, provided much more detailed and coherent guidance on children's basic needs at different ages, the interaction of these needs with parenting and with other environmental factors. Although there has been criticism of this guidance and the preceding work on looked after children, the expectation and hope was that this would lead to an improvement in social work practice. The familiar 'triangle' (see Figure 2.1) was particularly valuable in relation to the issue of neglect since it demonstrated the wide range of factors which affect children's well-being. However, the years following the publication of this guidance have seen significant concern and unrest in the profession about its application and implications. At this time, it is not clear that it has resulted in significant improvement in work with neglectful families and, more specifically, in the skills of observing and communicating with children in their birth families. What, then, is needed if the social worker is to re-establish his or her role in this key aspect of the work? Exhortations have failed, and guidance, though it has provided an orderly framework for the application of knowledge in the processes of assessment, has not reached the heart of the matter. Although this is of general concern, with implications for work with adults as well as children, it is of particular importance in relation to children. It makes a mockery of the law which places children's well-being as paramount if, as often seems to be the case, the weakest aspect of the work is in direct contact with them. Furthermore, as part of the recognition of children's rights, there is now much greater general emphasis on the importance of eliciting feelings, views and attitudes towards their circumstances.

It is obvious that children living at home who are in any way maltreated have rights to such consideration; it should not be assumed that these processes only begin with verbal interactions. The opportunities to observe and interact start much sooner. Youell (2005) provides a sensitive example of the interaction with 'a quiet baby', 'Kylie' of seven months, with a worker who was trying to engage her. She 'showed no response to sound or to movement' for some considerable time but then began to respond:

> 'At this moment I was interrupted for a few seconds by somebody at the door and when I turned back to Kylie it was as if she had switched off. She was staring blankly ahead and made no response when I spoke to her and took her hands again.' (Youell, 2005)

Youell comments:

> 'The idea that babies or toddlers might be so damaged as to fall into states of despair at a very young age is deeply abhorrent, particularly to social workers who feel impotent in the face of a shortage of resources or the absence of sufficient evidence to take action.' (Youell, 2005, p. 51)

There are six preconditions for lasting improvements in this sphere of work. Whilst they apply to all work with maltreated children, they are particularly important in cases such as serious neglect, which are, or should be long-term:

- Basic and post-qualifying education must include opportunities for students to apply and reflect upon their knowledge of child development, aided by sensitive supervision.
- Practitioners must also have opportunities to refine and consolidate these skills. They must also have opportunities for consultation.
- Both students and practitioners must be helped to examine the impact which direct contact with children (often disturbed or distressed) has upon them; this is not only to support them. It enables them, through greater awareness, to make more accurate assessments.
- Some work with children, especially when they are young, is carried out at children's centres, in which the workers may be qualified in other disciplines. They need similar skills and supervision. Social workers who do not have any supervisory role, but who keep closely in touch with those who work directly with children, have to acquire the skill of listening sensitively and interpreting the meaning of what is described.
- The difficulties of establishing contact with children when parents are ambivalent, anxious and hostile must be addressed in practical ways and recognition given to the anxieties raised in the workers.
- Whatever form of 'comprehensive assessment' is required, it must not result in false detachment and excessive preoccupation with 'categories' or 'tick boxes'. Completion of the process must not be

seen as a hurdle to be jumped before any effective care planning can be done. In cases of neglect, where there may be no crisis, but where parents do not cooperate, this can be disastrous.

The essence of this work with children lies in reacting to them, in experiencing them. The work of Clare Winnicott, so little used in recent years, cannot be bettered for its understanding of these issues (Kanter, 2004). No one in the British context has written more directly and with such clarity. On social workers and children she concludes:

'To sum up, I would say that if we believe in the reality of children's feelings, we shall not find it difficult to communicate. If, on the other hand, we do not have this belief, we cannot get round the difficulty by learning techniques. It is better then to leave alone the subject of communicating with children.' (Kanter, 2004, p. 197; Winnicott, 1964)

That remains the challenge.

Conclusion

This chapter has briefly outlined the foundations for healthy child development; the effects of serious neglect on development; specific difficulties with caregivers which impact on children; and the role of social workers in direct work with children.

Working Together in Cases of Neglect; Unresolved Problems and Current Issues

There is now a significant body of literature in the UK on the theme of 'working together' in the field of social care, much of it in relation to child protection. The issue has long been recognised by the government as critical for effective work. This was evident from 1950 (Home Office, 1950) but, from the late 1960s, and given greater urgency by the Maria Colwell inquiry (DHSS, 1974a), there was a steady stream of advice on this topic. Between 1974 (DHSS, 1974b) and 2006 (DfES, 2006), those involved in child protection have been required to follow extensive and prescriptive guidance on a wide range of topics related to the objectives and processes of working together. There is also a growing body of research to be considered later; most of it, however, is small scale and does not carry the authority of the earlier work of Birchall and Hallett (1995) and Hallett (1995).

There have also been a number of Serious Case Reviews, involving the death, or near death, of neglected children. Many of these reviews, commissioned by Area Child Protection Committees, have not received wide publicity or been generally available. However, for those in the field, they have contributed to a growing sense of unease at the failures of communication and cooperation which they reveal. More familiar in recent years and highly significant in the story of working together, have been the reviews on 'Paul' (The Bridge Consultancy, 1995), Victoria Climbié (Laming, 2003) and 'The W Family' (Cantrill, 2006). The death of Victoria Climbié was, of course, associated with gross physical abuse as well as neglect. That reminds us that serious neglect is often associated with other forms of abuse.

This chapter is in two parts. First, I shall discuss some aspects of the current situation generally, which are as pertinent to neglect as other forms of maltreatment. Second, I shall reflect on particular issues and difficulties which arise in working together with neglectful families.

The current situation

We lack the evidence to make a current appraisal of the quality in the UK of interagency and interprofessional work in child protection. There is demonstrable and stark evidence of failures in particular cases which have attracted wide attention. But it is several steps too far to use this as an indication of widespread failures. The introduction of joint audit for the new Local Children's Safeguarding Boards (LCSB), which replace Area Child Protection Committees, may go some way to providing reliable national evidence in England and Wales from the perspective of different agencies and professionals. But the complexity and subtlety of linking processes to outcomes is well known, not least because of the many variable factors which affect outcomes. It is important to acknowledge the effort, resources and commitment which have been put into improving the quality of working together. There is a real danger of fastening on conspicuous failures in individual cases and generalising from them.

There are, however, a number of concerns which may justifiably create anxiety that the working together edifice has weaknesses which place it in danger. First, and incontrovertibly, there have been severe shortages of personnel in some areas, especially social workers, which jeopardise efforts at cooperation. A degree of continuity in relationships is a prerequisite for effective working together. This is critically important in cases of neglect in which medium- or long-term work is essential. Second, at the present time we are, yet again, coping with major structural change, for example in the fields of primary health care and children's services, which brings together education and social services. Whatever the merits of the changes, it creates instability in the organisations; in particular it unsettles staff and increases mobility. Third, we await the rolling out of the new systems for a common database for children, which will include specifications of 'concerns', such as maltreatment. Previous experience does not inspire confidence that this process will be smooth and there is much controversy surrounding the plans, including matters surrounding confidentiality, in which child maltreatment creates particular tensions.

A fourth concern, as scrutiny of successive Working Together guidance referred to above clearly shows, is that the number and type of agencies and workers who are now expected to participate in protecting and safeguarding children has increased steadily over the years. This is both understandable and commendable. We are moving towards a society in which this is to be regarded as 'everybody's business'. But its implications in terms of organisation and training and therefore resources, are far reaching and complex.

Fifth, and related to this, some have expressed concern that the inclusiveness, but also the vagueness, of the term 'safeguarding', linked to the key concerns in *Every Child Matters* (DfES, 2004) will deflect attention from the still imperfect systems for effective cooperation in cases of child maltreatment.

Lastly, there is increasing criticism of the direction and emphasis of the official Working Together guidance and its effect on those required to implement it. Put bluntly, and perhaps simplistically, it is argued that the instrumental aspect of cooperative activity is not balanced by a recognition of the importance of its expressive aspects. That is to say, whilst it is important to put in place reliable systems for cooperation between professionals on assessment and intervention in child protection, there has also to be better understanding of the emotions involved in this kind of work and the effects this has on communication and cooperation between professionals. This has particular resonance in cases of serious neglect in which the feelings of confusion and despair are often quite intense in the workers.

This last area of concern has been forcefully articulated by a number of influential writers in this field. (See, for example, Reder & Duncan, 2003 and Cooper, 2005.) It has been reinforced by empirical research, such as that of Tresider *et al.* (2003), in a study of a multi-agency action research project to improve service delivery to families with complex needs, including those in which neglect loomed large. Focus groups with 72 professionals from a wide range of agencies were asked to identify the key challenges which they experienced. High on the agenda were the 'personal challenges' of the work:

> 'These challenges reflected the overwhelming nature of work with families enduring complex needs, the difficulty of separating the personal from the professional, as well as the impact of work on personal life. Vivid and difficult feelings were experienced. A related theme was the "management of compassion" and the difficulties associated with achieving a balance between emotional involvement and professional detachment. There was a struggle not to take problems home, which, as one worker put it, could become "like a haunting".' (Tresider *et al.*, 2003, p. 11)

Their work raises the key question – how can organisations which necessarily and properly run on principles of order and rationality take into account the underlying emotional dynamics which profoundly affect the behaviour of their staff, most especially when they are 'tasked' to protect and to safeguard children? Although these anxieties were being expressed before the Climbié inquiry took place, that event sharpened the current critique of government policy. Unless the 'rational' individual or organisation can accept, attempt to understand and use the emotions vested in this work, cooperative work will not be effective. These emotions should not be viewed in solely negative terms; they are the drivers of positive and negative behaviours and they underpin purposeful behaviour.

This takes us into the sphere of training, education and staff development. Many Area Child Protection Committees (ACPCs) have devoted much time and energy to education and training, both in awareness raising (though often in separate work groups), and multidisciplinary meetings on specific topics, including neglect. There is no reason to suppose that these will not be carried forward by the new Local Child Safeguarding Boards (LCSBs). The challenge is to find ways of encouraging reflection on the impact of child maltreatment on workers and on the interactions between them. Reder and Duncan (2003) offer a valuable illustration from the field of communication psychology.

However welcome such innovatory training may be, it has to be complemented by a recognition within agencies, especially through new forms of supervision or consultation, that there has to be 'reflective space' in which the interactions *between thinking and feeling* can be purposefully explored.

In recent years, there has been little development of these ideas within and between agencies, not least because of the urgency and pressure to implement messages from above about procedural improvements. This is appropriate, but it also can be a distraction from the deeper problems which arise in engaging constructively with others in the service of maltreated children and their families. Of course, this should be a rebalancing exercise, not a retreat from tackling difficult 'systemic' problems; there are real difficulties in holding together the range of complex issues which emerge in considering effective working together. The neglect of the 'expressive' dimension in this sphere of activity reflects more generally a limited understanding of the significance of emotions in professional interactions. But we have reached a stage when, unless this dimension is acknowledged and used constructively, calamities and tragedies, as well as 'near misses' (Bostock *et al.*, 2006) will continue to happen and case reviewers will continue to be baffled by the obvious flaws in interprofessional practice.

Examination of research (see, for example, Darlington *et al.*, 2005; Frost *et al.*, 2005) over recent years shows considerable consensus about the factors which are involved in effective communication and co-operation. In 1989, I suggested the following dimensions:

- Structure and systems.
- Relative status and perceived power of the parties.
- Excessive identification with role, i.e. with particular clients or aspects of their difficulties.
- Professional and organisational priorities.
- The extent and ways in which cooperation is perceived as mutually beneficial.
- The dynamics of case conferences (or, of course, other meetings of this kind).
- Differing attitudes towards and values concerning child abuse and the family. (Stevenson, 1989)

These factors recur again and again in later research, such as that discussed below. However, some expansion and modification is needed. For example, there needs to be an analysis of the concept of role which explores aspects beyond that of 'identification'. The ways in which workers define their roles and perceive them in relation to those held by others, and the understanding which each has of the other, has emerged as highly significant in the processes of interprofessional working. (See for example, Stanley et al., 2003; Darlington et al., 2005.) The phrase 'role identification', however, emphasises the extent to which it may affect the way workers perceive, and sometimes limit, the scope of their work. Role definitions foster professional security and clarity but they can also act as blinkers, restricting the vision of what needs to be done for the family as a whole. The most common examples are found with the adult mental health services, or those services for parents with learning disabilities, and child protection.

The omission of the issue of confidentiality in the early 'list' will also be noted. In the early years of the literature on interagency and interprofessional cooperation it seemed reasonable to suppose that conflicts over the exchange of information would be resolved by a better understanding of mutual roles and responsibilities, including legal duties. Government guidance was unequivocal on the primacy of 'the child's best interests'. Present plans for the introduction of a common assessment framework could be seen as consolidating this approach. However, we find ourselves in a climate of anxiety and fear about 'data protection' and about the dangers of litigation. It seems likely that, far from fading in importance, the next years will see some powerful conflicts around the matter of confidentiality which will have an impact on the general behaviour of professionals.

Thus, as was to be expected, the 'dimensions' identified in 1989 can only be used as a starting point for further elaboration. They have not been superseded. However, it was not made sufficiently explicit at that time that all these dimensions arouse strong feelings in those involved and these can impede working together. They set in train reactions and responses in which 'the personal and the professional' cannot be clearly distinguished and which can affect outcomes, both positively and negatively.

In summary: this section has identified areas of present difficulty in interagency and interprofessional working, all of which have a bearing on the way cases of serious neglect are handled. The final comment on the need for better understanding of the part played by emotions in interprofessional discourse has been emphasised. This is not to suggest it is the most important. Rather, it is to put emotions firmly on the agenda of those whose preoccupations with structures and systems may lead them to neglect (at their peril) the powerful undercurrents which threaten the foundations of the structures they seek to put in place (Cooper, 2005).

Issues and difficulties in relation to neglect

This section will consider certain specific difficulties which arise in cooperative work. They offer specific examples of the dimensions previously identified, for example in relation to status and power and narrow definitions of role, as well as more fundamental differences of attitude and belief.

The split between welfare and justice systems

In Chapter 4, it was argued that, since neglectful parenting may, and usually does, include inadequate discipline and supervision, it is unsurprising that a number of the children in these families exhibit antisocial and delinquent behaviour. Unfortunately, there is a kind of split in the way children are perceived – as needy or as a threat.

This tension underlies the debate on the best way to treat those who do not conform to social norms and values. It is made explicit in the judicial system of England and Wales in which there are two strands, those dealing with juvenile crime and those dealing with 'welfare' as embodied in the family courts. These often seem to run parallel courses, with little or no 'meeting of minds'. This issue is particularly significant at the present time. Its wider implications, including comparisons between nations are explored in Hill *et al.* (2006) which discusses a range of issues in child protection and youth justice. In the context of neglected children and working together, it is extremely important to recognise the deep divisions in values and attitudes which affect the ways in which such children are seen by society and which influence how they are treated within the judicial system.

Whilst there has been much general criticism of parents who neglect their parental duties of supervision and control, there has not been systematic application of this aspect of 'the neglectful syndrome' to child maltreatment. Although in the definition of neglect reference is made to 'failure to ensure adequate supervision' (DfES, 2006, 1.33), government guidance generally has not made a clear association between the situation of delinquent children and those who are seriously neglected in their homes, who are often inadequately supervised by their parent(s).

In the first edition of this book, reference was made to the attitudes of the police towards neglect. In Birchall and Hallett (1995) and Hallett (1995), in which different professionals commented on vignettes, the police viewed 'neglect' as being primarily about 'dirt'. We are familiar with descriptions of such households. This reflects the circumstances in which police often become involved. However, police may be called to homes for the more tangible 'incident-based' events including domestic violence; even when these are not substantiated or sufficiently serious to require action, it is important for the level of awareness of neglect as a wider concept than 'low hygiene' to be raised. Such families are often well known in the neighbourhood. Police may have much more useful information to share (often derived from acquaintance with juvenile offenders) than a simplistic and limited 'incident investigation'. Indeed, they may have more of a role in intervention than first appears. There has been a worrying split in our thinking between the juvenile 'victims' and juvenile 'villains' which fails to connect the indications of lack of care and control at home (an aspect of neglect) with some youthful tyrants who dominate the streets or their 'hangers-on'.

Since the Birchall and Hallett research in the mid-1990s, youth justice services in England and Wales have developed and are now central to the provision for delinquent children and young people. We have relatively little evidence as yet on the 'working together' of child protection and youth services but initial findings are discouraging (Bottoms & Kemp, 2006). Bottoms and Kemp examine the post-1998 youth justice system and its impact. They discuss the extent to which 'welfare issues' are addressed by Youth Justice Teams. They refer to repeated criticisms that have been made of the lack of cooperation between the 'two sides' – youth justice and child protection services, most recently by the Audit Commission in 2004. Their own small-scale research gives illustrations from two cases in which youth justice workers approached their work very differently, in terms of the balance between welfare and justice issues. The first worker wished to restrict her role to justice, i.e. seeking to focus only on the offence; the second worker 'sought to get involved in the welfare issues' (p. 152).

These cases illustrate the profound difficulties which are created by underlying unresolved ideological conflict. They do not simply arise because there are two systems; the systems are created to reflect two ideologies which seem actually or potentially incompatible. Workers get trapped in these situations and seek to manage their own feelings by a variety of strategies and by considerable variation in role.

Bottoms and Kemp conclude their discussion with reference to the creation of Children's Centres. The hope is that this will facilitate better working together at the front line. However, it is clear 'that the Home Office expects the youth justice systems to be distinct from the child care system' (Home Office, 2004, p. 9). The Youth Justice Board has also issued guidance that 'YOTs [Youth Offending Teams] must not be so embedded within the child welfare system that the confidence, support and contribution of criminal justice agencies and the public is lost' (YJB, 2004, p. 6).

What is so unfortunate about these comments is that they seem to assume that there is a necessary separation between justice and welfare in terms of service provision. A recent survey of family centres from 1995 onwards (Tunstill *et al.*, 2007) did not find connections between delinquency services and the work of the centres. In this aspect of the work, there are formidable barriers to achieving effective working together. Families in which there are older neglected children are ill-served by such dichotomies.

Neglected children and the family courts

Despite the extensive evidence on the significant harm caused to children by serious neglect, there remain many doubts in the minds of practitioners as to whether or when to take action through the courts. There can, of course, be agonising decisions in which the future lives of children at home or 'looked after' are at stake. That fundamental choice will always be, and should be, a matter for the most serious deliberation. However, it seems that the discourse between different professionals and the relationship with the judiciary complicate and sometime distort the processes necessary to reach a conclusion. Also, it appears that the situation has not improved since the first edition of this book. The difficulties have been admirably set out by Iwaniec *et al.* (2004), the title of whose article 'The plight of neglected children' indicates their grave concern about the present position. They argue:

> 'When and how to intervene in cases of child neglect, poses a dilemma not only for social work, but also for the legal profession. To social workers, legal decision making about neglect may

appear to favour the carer over the child. Equally, to lawyers, social workers may appear to allow the cases of neglect to drift from bad to worse for years, at times hoping that parents will change and improve the quality of their child care, because they said so, or because the neglect is associated with structural circumstances and situations at times beyond their control.

If a case of neglect eventually reaches court, there may be overwhelming evidence of harm to the child, and, as a result, the judiciary and, indeed, the children's guardians, may be at a loss to understand why the case was not brought sooner so the harm could have been limited. Whilst this state of affairs may be a source of judicial criticism, it may also be a source of frustration among social workers who have to deal with conflicting issues (such as the rights of the child versus the rights of the parents, and the principle of minimal intervention). Reaching a decision that neglect has attained a level of significant harm can be something to be avoided rather than confronted. At times, neglect cases appear to engender professional paralysis in terms of taking legal action to protect the child.' (Iwaniec *et al.*, 2004)

Their findings, from research in Northern Ireland (Donaldson, 2004), identify a range of problems which arise when social workers and lawyers meet over neglect cases. Many of these arise from weaknesses in the practice of professionals The authors do not suggest there is, or need be, an unbridgeable gulf between the judiciary and social workers in the way the concept of neglect and its effects are viewed, but they demonstrate a clear need for better understanding.

One element in the judicial process concerns thresholds at which significant harm in cases of neglect is reached. There has been an almost obsessive preoccupation with 'thresholds' amongst social workers and their managers, reflecting a need to find the equivalent of an 'incident' in other types of abuse, in order to set court processes in train. However, it is noticeable that recently there has been less emphasis on thresholds, for example in the latest government guidance (DfES, 2006). What is needed is interagency and interprofessional recognition that, whilst sound evidence of the harmful effects of neglect is essential, in the end decisions about action are matters of cumulative judgement about individual families and particular children. There can be no generalised thresholds.

If neglect is found to be proven, there remains a crucial decision concerning parental capacity to improve the care of their children. Judges and magistrates are unlikely to be better equipped than the child welfare professionals to form a judgement on this, and the views of those who have seen parents over longer periods and in the home situation should sometimes carry more weight. The courts are, of course, assisted by their guardians, who will be social workers. The interactions between local authority social workers and guardians are sometimes problematic. It is important, especially in complicated neglect cases, that the experience of working with families over time should be taken into account as well as the particular expertise of guardians. In this matter all parties may be caught up to varying degrees in balancing the welfare of children with the legal requirement to work with parents and, in particular, sympathy with some neglectful parents. Whilst not documented systematically, there seems to be at least anecdotal evidence of occasions in which there have been protracted and doomed efforts at rehabilitation, in which vital years of children's development have been lost in the vain hope of improvement in their care.

If and when the time comes for the children to be removed, the care proposed will be the subject of judicial scrutiny. The most likely area of conflict between the social services and the courts is the matter of continuing contact with parents. This is an issue which goes beyond neglected children to child welfare policy generally, and is of the utmost importance. From observation and anecdote, as well as reported cases from the higher courts, it is evident that considerable conflict surrounds such decisions and further research and study are much needed. However, as we shall discuss in the final chapter of this book, models of shared care, with or without court orders, might profitably be developed with those neglectful parents whose parenting capacity seems irreparably damaged but who have established relationships with the children and have love to offer them. It is to be hoped that such arrangements can be fostered by the courts.

There is an important aspect of the interface between lawyers and social workers, that of relationships *within* social services, which has recently been the subject of a study by Dickens (2006; 2007). This explores the ways that local authority social workers, social service managers and lawyers work together in child care cases in England. Part of that work was an examination of the cases which involved neglect. Dickens concludes that the relationship between these three groups is fraught:

> 'The different responsibilities, priorities and practices of each group sometimes coincide and at other times compete. Social workers, especially the less experienced, tend to be grateful for any help they can get from the lawyer; but managers may resent this as excessive and over intrusive, and the lawyers themselves complained of being pulled too far into social work matters and support. The relationship between . . . managers and lawyers is particularly problematic.' (Dickens 2007)

Dickens' findings raise issues wider than the focus of this book. However, his analysis of the neglect cases (Dickens, 2007) throws light on hitherto unexplored aspects of interprofessional work. The sample of 23 cases included 12 in which neglect could be considered as a significant factor and it was a lesser factor in 7; that is, neglect was a problem in 19 out of 23 cases. There were also comments about neglect from the interviewees in response to general questions.

The title of Dickens' article 'Child neglect and the law: catapults, thresholds and delay' aptly summarises its main themes. He shows that the local authority lawyers wanted to find a 'catapult' in order to take action. The notion of needing a catapult is crucial, not just to speed up the action of the courts:

'Before that, the legal department will have to agree to support an application to court and social services will have to authorise (expensive) legal proceedings . . . The catapult might be a specific event, a change of circumstances or (*but much, much less often*) an accumulation of concerns.' (Dickens, 2007)

Delay is also discussed. 'The wait for a decisive event combined with the difficult practice and ethical questions' results in delay. There are also factors in the lives of the families which can contribute to this. For example, if a new family member, probably a partner, arrives, the situation may need to be reassessed. It is also inherent in the nature of intractable neglect cases that there may be delays in obtaining the necessary information, such as that for a family assessment.

Dickens also points to delays when, from a lawyer's viewpoint, the family 'only just cooperates' and this makes it hard for social services to start proceedings. This may lead to a series of delays whilst efforts are made to appraise the situation. It is also depressingly evident that, without 'the catapult', usually evidence of a conventionally forensic nature, the professionals feel impotent to act. The picture is one of considerable tension and, at times, resentment between this triangle of professionals.

Dickens' research gives little ground for optimism that there is improving official understanding of the cumulative effects of neglect on the developing child, within the agencies and institutions which hold the responsibility for, and the power over, children's lives, although individual professionals may be keenly aware of it. He suggests that this is inevitable in the context of an adversarial system in the courts. The issue is further complicated when there are strained relations between social workers and the courts.

If we read across from the work of Iwaniec *et al.* (2004) to that of Dickens (2007), it becomes apparent that, although the case for neglect as profoundly important in causing 'significant harm' to children has been made and is accepted by those with knowledge and influence in social services, other agencies and the courts, there is still confusion and doubt in the minds of many who have to operate in day-to-day practice. There are also many impediments to putting the knowledge into practice. In fairness, it must be acknowledged that the evidence about parental capacity to change is much less secure than the evidence of the harm neglect may cause. This fact, plus the underlying doubts about effectiveness, create some of the tensions which arise between professionals. This may suggest the need for radical changes in policy which might free us from the 'children at home' versus 'children away' model to which we are accustomed. The final chapter will take this further.

Multidisciplinary work; adult and children's services

As we have seen, the factors which lie behind the neglect of children are many and diverse, and interact with each other. We have also seen how frequently certain parental difficulties arise, in particular, mental health problems, including substance abuse and those which may arise from learning disabilities. Recent research suggests that especially in our fragmented social work services, social workers lack confidence in their expertise in particular spheres of their work. Thus, Taylor and Kroll (2004) refer to the uncertainty which statutory drug workers expressed about assessing parenting and children's well-being, whilst child protection workers felt similarly about the effects of substance abuse. Darlington *et al.* (2005), writing in an Australian context, refer to the difficulties experienced by child protection workers in assessing risk to children in relation to mentally ill parents.

Pearce (2003) describes a process of training which attempts to address these issues:

> 'It has become clear during the mid-90s that social work practitioners rapidly perceived themselves as deskilled as generic social workers . . . The separation of services with adult care, mental health and child care has led to a distancing of workers from each other, with a consequent lack of understanding.' (Pearce, 2003, pp. 114–115)

This leads us into the complex territory of genericism and specialisation in social work, as well as interprofessional cooperation more generally (Stevenson, 2005a). I have argued that a holistic approach to the child's well-being, and an ecological approach in understanding why the neglect has arisen, are integral to effective work. It follows, therefore, that knowledge and the associated skills will be drawn from many different sources. Some of these will be found in the disciplines of different professions; this means that part of working together must involve the sharing of knowledge. At a day-to-day level, this is easier said than done; there are various reasons why such basic exchanges are not achieved. For example, workers may feel inhibited about admitting that they do not understand certain aspects of parental mental illness and its implications; others may appear not to value the knowledge and understanding which their colleagues have of the family. (Status considerations are relevant here.) Meetings may take place in an atmosphere of tension and haste, in which the opportunity to learn from each other is not taken.

Clearly, this is an area in which education and training has a crucial role to play and one in which LCSBs are particularly important. Specific kinds of *risk to the child from neglect* should be related to knowledge about certain types of emotional or mental disorder or disability in the parent(s). For example, Murphy and Harbin (2003), add to the familiar 'assessment framework' triangle (DoH, 2000) to highlight issues surrounding substance abuse (see Appendix 5). Thus, against the side of the triangle concerning parenting capacity, they add questions that need to be asked if parents are drug abusers: what substance, how much, etc.? They also ask about the potential impact of such abuse on all family members. The risk to children can then be evaluated in more detail.

If similar applications are made in which other parental problems or 'deficits' are specifically linked to the child's developmental needs, these could offer starting points for more specific exchanges between workers. For example, an understanding of the impact of current depression on a mother can be related to the attachment needs of an infant or the capacity of an older child to cope with it. This raises two questions. What basic knowledge of parents *and* children should all individual professionals have who work with families in which there is serious child neglect? How can we ensure that the expertise is shared and made available in cooperative working? There are difficulties about sharing. The current divisions, both organisationally and professionally, lead to definition of roles which are focused on individuals as the unit of concern, rather then the family. At a personal level, work perceived as centring on a particular individual member can lead to an emotional preoccupation with that person to the exclusion of others. In particular, the division between adults' and children's services, recently increased by structural change, can create serious conflicts of interest within the professional group.

These tensions are exacerbated in child protection because the law places the children's 'best interests' first. Thus, there are cases in which certain actions to protect the child may adversely affect a parent, for example a depressed mother might become suicidal, or there may be fears of this happening. Such situations are bound to occur from time to time, but present structures may work against the sensitive management of the case and of its impact on workers. There are so many issues to be raised and discussed; for example, all workers need to recognise that the ultimate tragedy for a parent is to be responsible (by commission or omission) for the death of a child. Workers 'on each side' of the adult/child divide need to have trust in the knowledge which the other is using to support their concerns. (Do they fear that there is exaggeration of the 'significant harm' through neglect? Or that there is minimisation of the impact of parental problems on their capacity to care?)

Can we therefore create more effective and focused structures to work with these families? The persisting reports of difficulties in working together in cases of serious maltreatment, including serious neglect, indicate that we have not found satisfactory models. The need for multidisciplinary teams was acknowledged in *Every Child Matters* (DfES, 2003, p. 5). There is a variety in operation across the country. However, there do not appear to be many attempts to construct such teams on the basis of the family as a unit of referral which would thus combine workers from both adult and children's services. There will be bureaucratic and professional obstacles to such innovations. But perhaps the time has come to acknowledge that, in certain types of particularly complex work, including serious neglect of children, which involve tensions between the interests of parents and children, there is no other way to achieve effective working together.

The argument rests on five key points:

- The distinctive feature of such a team will be to represent the interests of both adults and children and to offer a forum in which to work out conflicts of interest when they arise.
- In some cases, including those involving serious neglect, consistent and regular work with families over a substantial period of time is a prerequisite for effective intervention.
- Such cases will usually require 'packages' of care which involve a number of workers with different knowledge and expertise. Their mutual understanding and collaboration is also a prerequisite for effective intervention.
- The nature of this work is so difficult and demanding that it would not be reasonable to expect workers to commit to it indefinitely. A period such as three years might be considered. The notion of a temporary 'secondment' with guaranteed return to other types of service provision might be built in.
- The core team would be small but there should be clear links back into agencies, consultation and support built into the arrangements.

The construction of a core team cannot hope to include the entire range of professional expertise needed; the range and diversity of the problems particular cases present is too great. Thus, a possible way to construct this network of 'cooperating professionals' would be to think in terms of an inner and outer circle. The inner circle, the core team, must include a social worker with child protection expertise, a health visitor, and (possibly part-time) workers in adult mental health services, including substance abuse, or those with learning disability expertise, according to the nature of the case. There will also be a need to include those who work directly with the family on specific problems such as those in Children's Centres.

The role of designated community paediatricians is of particular importance in work with neglected children. Their approach is certain to be holistic and they are recognised nationally as key players in both assessment and planning. If it is not feasible to include them in a core team, they should be integral to some aspects of the team's work, including an element of leadership in the chairing of meetings and, perhaps, in the management of conflict.

The core team must have an outer circle of experts with a formal and explicit route to them when required. That is to say, the professionals in the outer circle must accept some responsibility for the work of the team, whether as advisors or in sharing some direct work with the families. These arrangements are key to the success of the project. Crucial to the outer circle would be: mental health professionals, including adult psychiatrists; 'educationalists' (i.e. teachers/psychologists); debt advisors; youth justice workers, police and CAMHS.

This discussion is only intended as an illustration of a possible model and a springboard for further debate which would take local variations into account. There are many conundrums, including the extent to which part-time workers could be used without invalidating the concept of close working partnerships. There needs to be a systematic introduction of different patterns of working more closely. One issue is the justification for singling out serious neglect as the specific trigger for such experiments. Tresider *et al.* (2003) refer to the possibility of bringing multidisciplinary teams together around a certain kind of specific issue; they call these 'virtual teams' (p. 24). Their suggestions do not focus on neglect per se and will not address the need for consistent, long-term working. Their ideas do, however, emphasise the need for the 'outer circle' of available experts.

Much will depend on local circumstances, including, of course, the numbers of cases of serious neglect in particular neighbourhoods. There may be argument for establishing such teams with a remit wider than that for 'neglectful families'. The criteria, however, are clear; they must be cases requiring intensive and protracted intervention and ones in which the relationship between adult and children's services is critical.

The role of the school

The role of the school in contributing to the support of neglected children is very important. Teachers are not the only staff who can be involved. For example, in some areas, the school nurse may play an important part. The potential role of education welfare officers, especially in those cases of neglect which involve poor school attendance, is obvious, although there is little research to illuminate what part they are actually playing. It is not clear whether the current emphasis on the improvement of school attendance is sufficiently linked in to 'safeguarding' work for neglected children.

The role of educational psychologists is also highly significant in cases of neglected children, whose educational attainments are so often below average. It is probably generally accepted that the concern of teachers about sexual and physical abuse has been more explicit than about neglect, especially in relation to anxiety about the impact of formal referral on their pupils. Yet, in discussion, it often emerges that teachers are deeply worried about neglected children and, in primary schools especially, there are often moving accounts of the efforts which they have made to supplement poor care at home with 'unofficial' help about cleanliness and comfort, including food.

The grave and long-term effects of neglect on cognitive development are established. The increasingly competitive emphasis on school tests and results, and the judgements that are made about schools on the basis of this work must be balanced against the creation of a climate in which damaged children can be nurtured and stimulated intellectually. It will be sad if political emphasis on improving standards and on reducing 'social exclusion' generally results in neglect of the very children who will not improve without special attention. It is appreciated that many of these matters are not within the control of the schools and the teachers in them. Their involvement in child protection systems has been complicated by the devolution of responsibility from local education authorities to local governors, with the associated problems of prioritising expenditure. The task of local education departments in coordinating child protection arrangements has also been made much more difficult by these arrangements.

Since the first edition of the book was published, research (Bakinsky, 2000; 2003) has reinforced concern about the position of teachers in the safeguarding network; she drew attention to inadequacies in the training of teachers. In her first survey, teachers themselves drew attention to the need for more training in 'identification and action when emotional abuse, neglect or "failure to thrive" is suspected' (p. 36). Bakinsky concludes, after a second survey, that pre-service and regular in-service training (in child protection) may be desirable. She concludes: 'As controversial as such a requirement might prove . . . it may be what is required to make sure schools really are in a position to be part of a joined-up multi-agency approach which does protect children' (p. 127).

At present, there is renewed debate about the place of special schools in educational provision. The now familiar arguments about 'normalisation' and avoidance of stigma are put forward against the possible benefits of a specialised educational regime. This issue cannot be explored here. It is, however, beyond doubt that many school-age children from seriously neglectful families require a degree of 'nurturing' at school well beyond that available to most schoolchildren. For these children, in their day-to-day lives, school may be the only warm and safe place and they can only learn when they are warm and safe. Whether they are in mainstream or special schools, the school is pivotal. Yet these are the children who are likely to be poor in attendance, unpopular with other children (and perhaps staff). Their needs are not generally well served in the present arrangements.

Intra-agency work; continuing difficulties in integrating health care

Working together *within* the health services is of particular relevance to children in neglectful families; there is often inadequate attention paid by parents to their health needs. One of the key roles is that of the general practitioner in the child protection system. The position of general practitioners in the child protection system has long been considered unsatisfactory by other participants (Hallett & Stevenson, 1980). There are complex difficulties underlying this which we have not been successful in addressing in more than 20 years. GPs' 'severity ratings' of neglect in Birchall and Hallett (1995) were not strikingly different from other professional colleagues, although they tended to be at the lower end of the scale. They did not see neglect differently from other forms of abuse in terms of severity. However, in a questionnaire administered to a large sample, Birchall and Hallett found that 'there is a lot of dissatisfaction around general practitioners' role'. Few found them very easy to work with – especially social workers and police. 'Two thirds of paediatricians and health visitors think they perform poorly' (in the field of child protection) (Birchall & Hallett, 1995, p. 237).

Hallett concludes, on the basis of both studies, that 'the mandate to work together is not widely accepted by general practitioners, who may have the status and independence to ignore it'. She suggests that they may in fact have 'little to contribute' (p. 333), but points out that 90% of those interviewed considered the GP's role to be 'essential' or 'important' in child protection and that there are striking exceptions to these criticisms. We have understood for a long time (Hallett & Stevenson, 1980) that general practitioners, amongst some other professionals, may feel themselves on the 'outer circle' of child protection, seeing very few cases and without a clear role in ongoing work. However, it is important that these problems in establishing the general practitioner within the child protection network should be resolved if the issue of neglect is to be tackled more effectively and systematically. Their importance rests not only on the occasions when clinical judgement needs to be exercised but also as leader of the primary health care team. Such leadership is of particular importance in cases of neglect. For, in such cases, there are sometimes complicating medical problems in the children; the interaction of these with lack of effective parental care is often highly problematic.

I have commented elsewhere (Stevenson, 2005b) that:

'There is ample evidence from serious case reviews, of which 'Paul' (The Bridge Consultancy, 1995) is perhaps the best known, that neglectful families have often subverted the best efforts of health professionals to provide care. In the case of Paul, no fewer than 13 health professionals and agencies were involved. More recently, my own experience, in relation to a review involving children with learning disabilities, has brought home to me the complex physical health needs many such children have.

The underlying reasons for the difficulties experienced in seeking to provide for the health needs of neglected children are not difficult to find. Yet, overcoming them has so far proved intractable. Neglectful parents, especially those with a number of children near in age, often have difficulty meeting the diverse health needs of their children. Characteristically, they do not keep appointments. It is common for the children to have a range of health-related problems, some of which may in themselves be caused or exacerbated by parental mismanagement. Thus, there may be a downward spiral, in which children become more ill, "poorly" and difficult to manage, and parents more desperate to avoid blame.

The families tend to be involved with a number of health professionals situated in various agencies: different hospitals, different outpatient departments; primary health care teams; a range of community health services, including those for schools, and so on. There can be a large number of individual practitioners with some direct responsibility. Some children have relatively minor problems, such as squints or (in Down's Syndrome) weak ankles; others have more serious and potentially grave problems, such as speech delay, which can adversely affect the child's future career at school. Health professionals have distinct identities and very different roles, and often have little or no contact with each other. Furthermore, they may not have shared governance.

The present system is meant to ensure that the general practitioner will receive notification of hospital outpatients' appointments, including "did not attend" notes (DNAs). But there is little to suggest that such information is followed up or collected in any systematic way. Sadly, these DNAs often only rise to the surface when a serious case review is undertaken. In any case, contact with health professionals is not restricted to such formalised appointments.

It would seem imperative to devise a method within the framework of health agencies by which such information could be systematically brought together and its cumulative significance assessed. Even the bare facts of attendance and non-attendance at health appointments over, for example, the course of a year would be invaluable. Leaving aside the obvious value of the health information per se, it would give important indications of the parents' capacity to handle the problems. The neglect of children's health needs can be a key factor in overall assessment.' (Stevenson, 2005b)

Research into the role of the general practitioner in safeguarding children, with specific reference to 'conflicts of interest' has been commissioned by the DfES (2006) and is under way at Kingston University. This is most welcome; it is to be hoped that the findings will include some focus on seriously neglected children, for in such cases, when not brought to a head by 'an incident', the general practitioner and health visitor in the primary health care team may have a critical contribution.

Conclusion

This chapter has addressed three broad areas:

- The general difficulties in ensuring good enough working together in the protection and safeguarding of children at the present time.

The part played by emotional dynamics and interactions is emphasised.
- Issues relating particularly to neglected children. These include the split between welfare and justice approaches; the interaction between the judicial system and social services; the tension between adult mental health and children's services; the role of schools.
- Intra-agency work: difficulties in integrating health care services.

We have to face up to the fact that interagency and interprofessional work, essential in cases of serious neglect, has on too many occasions failed to reach an adequate standard. Current changes and developments, however valuable in general, do not give confidence that these deficiencies will be addressed.

So What Is To Be Done?

As the previous chapters have shown, the past decade has seen a substantial increase in the literature on serious neglect as an aspect of child maltreatment. There is now soundly based evidence of its harmful effects and much well-founded discussion of the interlocking problems which give rise to it. However, there are two critical issues which are as yet imperfectly understood. These are:

- The factors which indicate parental capacity can be improved to achieve adequate care for their children.
- The models of intervention which are most likely to be effective.

This chapter will address those questions. But we must first ask: *why* is it important in terms of national policy and practice? Since the first edition of this book, there have been major government initiatives, notably Sure Start, which have aimed to address the problems of disadvantaged families and to intervene in families at an earlier stage than those discussed in this book. In cold logic, one might argue that policies directed to early prevention and support would be more beneficial to society than concentrating more attention and resources on a small number of highly dysfunctional families. However, this is not a realistic policy assumption for a number of reasons. First, although the numbers are small, families similar to these have been identified by the present government as 'high cost/high harm'; the actual expense of (often many) years to the State is very considerable. The adult lives of such children are very likely to be 'high cost' to the State. Second, preliminary evaluation of the Sure Start programmes suggests that they have been more helpful to families who are *less* disadvantaged than those discussed in this book. This may indicate that a different route may need to be taken if 'our' families are to be helped. Their continuing social exclusion has been noted and is the subject of specific government attention. For example, consultations hosted by the DfES and Treasury respectively have been entitled 'Families caught in a cycle of low achievement', 'High cost high harm families'.

Third, although the numbers are relatively small, families whose behaviour attracts public opprobrium and media attention raise political anxiety and may result in policy responses which are unhelpful. Earlier discussion (in Chapter 4) of the position of delinquent school-aged children living in neglectful families can be an example of this. They also sour local community relations. This is a problem which politicians cannot ignore. A small number of families can create much difficulty, distress and anger in local neighbourhoods when their behaviour impacts negatively on the lives of ordinary people. The urge to 'move them on', as seen in some television programmes, may be a relief to those in the vicinity but it leaves the underlying difficulties unresolved.

Fourth, and, in my view, of paramount importance there is a moral imperative underlying this work. Its justification lies not simply in children's value as social investments for the future, important as that is. It is unacceptable that we should have a sizeable group of children cut off from the normal decencies of life in Britain today. This is an issue about children's rights, as in the well-publicised government objective to design services for children which enable them to:

- 'Be healthy.
- Stay safe.
- Achieve economic well-being.
- Enjoy and achieve.
- Make a contribution.' (DfES, 2003)

On every count, many of the children here considered are not going, or are unlikely, to achieve these goals. Their daily life is miserable. I am reminded of a four-year-old boy, who, when asked what he liked about his new foster home, said: 'I like having my very own toothbrush and a clean bed.'

The Prime Minister, Tony Blair, addressing the issue of social exclusion in a speech in 2006, focused on the 'deeply intractable' aspects of the problem (Blair, 2006). He referred to those families who 'are very hard to reach' and whose difficulties are 'multiple, entrenched and often passed down the generations' (p. 1). The Prime Minister was well advised to qualify the last phrase by the word 'often' since this is a long-standing and contentious issue. However, formal recognition of a group of families and their characteristics who, if not identical to the families considered here, are very similar is an important step. Furthermore, the speech gives many examples of constructive intervention targeted at these families.

However, there is no denying how difficult it is to intervene effectively. This leads us back to the two critical issues.

Improving parenting capacity; the prognosis

There is so much that we do not yet understand. Also, 'change', for better or for worse, in the care offered to neglected children is affected by systems inside and outside the family. The departure or death of a close relative in the wider family; the onset of racial harassment; the arrival of a new class teacher; the allocation of a new dwelling; all these and many other factors have the potential to alter the existing situation. They are, of their nature, unpredictable. They cannot be taken into account in assessing the possibility of 'likely significant harm' to the children in the future. For practical purposes, therefore, it is the past and present behaviour of parents, usually the mother, which, in neglect cases, will form the basis of decisions about the future safety of our children. Gaudin (1993) points out that most measures of risk have not differentiated neglect from abuse, but cites Baird and Neufeldt (1988) as an exception. In their studies, they assessed the likelihood of continued neglect in relation to 550 families referred for neglect over a 12-month period. The factors which they drew out included:

- Caretaker neglected as a child.
- Single caretaker at time of referral.
- Caretaker history of drug/alcohol abuse.
- Age of youngest caretaker at time of referral.
- Number of children at home (i.e. more children increases the likelihood of neglect).
- Caretaker involved in primarily negative social relationships.
- Low motivation for change on part of caretaker.

This analysis does not throw any light on the effects of intervention. Sadly, however, it will not come as a surprise to British practitioners, who will be able to recollect such families without difficulty.

A depressing picture is painted by Crittenden (1988), who also distinguishes between abusing and neglecting caretakers and finds grounds for much more optimism about the former. She concludes that 'neglecting parents . . . have a very poor prognosis for improvement with treatment' (p. 184). There are several reasons for this:

> 'Neglectful parents tend to be limited intellectually, to have little concept of what is missing from their approach to child rearing and to be embedded in a social system that is materially and socially impoverished. Most important, they do not believe that others can effectively promote change. Thus, they lack skills, goals, resources and motivation . . . More than anything, they lack a belief in the efficacy of their own efforts.' (Crittenden, 1988, p. 184)

This is a gloomy picture indeed, and it is well supported by evidence. There seem to be three implications to be drawn from such findings. First, it is unhelpful to seriously neglected children to be optimistic about the likelihood of significant change in the behaviour of their caretakers. In particular, one must beware of the emotional investment in success and over-identification with parents, which has been a feature of such cases. Second, however, the judgement that caretakers will not improve sufficiently and in time does not inexorably lead to the removal of the children, although, on occasion, this will be inevitable. Rather, it may lead us to more realistic plans for the children in various domains of their lives. As Crittenden remarks: 'regardless of the parents' responsiveness to treatment, neglected children need preventative intervention' (p. 184). Third, however, as in all child abuse, there is no predictive tool which can adequately take account of the varying circumstances, life events and differing capacities of individuals to assure a given outcome. It must be remembered that these findings reflect, not only the intrinsic difficulties of the parents, but also the limitations of our present knowledge about ways to help.

Much of the recent debate about safeguarding and protection has been dominated by the topic of assessment. Unfortunately, the excellent foundation laid in the basic guidance (DoH, 2000a) seems to have been undermined by a preoccupation with the details of the process, which has been experienced as oppressive by practitioners. It remains to be seen how this will be resolved. Nonetheless, as discussed in Chapter 5, the familiar 'triangle' (see Figure 2.1) is a particularly good place to start in relation to seriously neglectful families. The 'parenting capacity' side of the triangle is a key area for detailed work, with the possibility of 'bolting on' other kinds of information. There are six basic prerequisites for a 'good enough' assessment of parental capacity to change:

- Knowledge of available evidence on specific effects of parental difficulties on child rearing, for example, learning disability, substance abuse.

- Ongoing regular appraisal of the situation, with the focus on 'significant harm'. (Assessment can never be 'finished'. Families, perhaps especially families like these, are in a constant state of flux.)
- Realistic appraisal of parents' will to change. (Past experience shows that the lack of the will to change, hidden or shown through hostility, has been a factor in misjudgements by workers.)
- Realistic appraisal of what is required in a given family to achieve 'good enough parenting'. (A 'step-by-step' approach to improvement may mask the fact that the journey is too long or difficult for the children's developmental timescales.)
- Identification of individual children's needs, deficits and strengths to lead to a better understanding of the importance of particular domains of parental capacity. (There has to be a crossover between the two.)
- The impact of poverty on the parents should be included as an integral part of the assessment. (It is not 'a context'; it is inseparable from the other stresses of daily living and has implications for the nature of interaction.)

'The big decision'

Children here considered are living in conditions so far below the acceptable norms that workers are bound to consider whether they can remain at home. As we have earlier discussed (in Chapter 5), this leads into the problematic area of court intervention. One of the key difficulties, well known, but not resolved, concerns timescales. Are delays increasing the likelihood of significant harm to the children? The disjunction between judicial processes and children's developmental needs has been long criticised (Goldstein *et al.*, 1996). (Of course, there is also much evidence of other kinds of harmful delay in the social services system itself.) There are two aspects to this; one concerns the management of court business, the other, the (understandable) caution which is exercised in reaching a decision to remove children.

On the first point, even when court business leading up to decisions on care orders runs smoothly, the time involved bears little relation to timescales in child development. The recent judicial protocol (Lord Chancellor's Department, 2005) for this process sets the target for the final hearing at 40 weeks after the first application. (The judge is given a further 20 days to make his/her findings.) In effect, then, if all goes well, it will take a year for this to take its course. Furthermore, in recent years there have been some deplorable delays and much longer periods of uncertainty, some of which have been due to the chequered beginnings of the new body, CAFCASS (Children and Families Court

Advisory and Support Services), set up in 2000; great difficulties were experienced by the courts in receiving a reliable and timely service for guardians.

Given the uncertainties about parental capacity to change, interim care orders may be used to see what progress can be made. Unfortunately, this can mean that children do not receive adequate care at certain vital stages in their development. Such decisions will be very difficult. It may be that clear connections between specific aspects of parenting and the developmental stages of the children can be made so that at least the dangers of delays are faced. For example, when parents are drug abusers and their lifestyle is characterised by a desperate search for drugs, the impact on children under two, in terms of cognitive stimulation and emotional bonding (in fact inseparable), must be a major source of concern, unless clear plans for alternative care are in place. In fact, this can lead to particular elements in the interim care plans, designed to offer some compensatory care appropriate to these developmental stages. However, there may be situations in which the deficits are so great, and parental capacity to change so uncertain, that delay in removing children seems more like procrastination than genuine uncertainty.

The tragic irony of this is that when these damaged children eventually leave home, their chances of successful fostering are diminished. This, combined with major concerns about the well-being of older children in the care system, means that we place some at double jeopardy by our delay. This may sound harsh; the plight of the parents is, in some cases, tragic. Such feelings are legitimate; this is why it is so difficult to follow the legal duty to act in 'the best interests of the child'. They cannot, however, be allowed to cloud judgements. Excessive doubts and confusion about the nature of developmental harm, as compared, for example, with that caused by physical violence, may combine with these emotions to result in damaging outcomes for children.

Case reviewers have also revealed situations in which workers have been unsure how to act when parents are hostile or (possibly) untruthful. Delays have resulted from difficulties in getting to see the children. Such reviewers often reveal anxious impotence before the tragic outcome. There is no doubt that workers need more help in coping with their fears and doubts. However, the legal position further compounds the uncertainty. Where there are no clear grounds for the making of an Emergency Protection Order, two possibilities for gaining access to the children currently exist. The first is under Section 46 of the Children Act 1989, by which police are able to remove and detain a child for up to 72 hours without reference to the court. This is not widely used and unless there is a manifest risk to young children, it may be difficult to use. However, it may also reflect uncertainty and excessive caution when past history, or what is known about the current circumstances, is not adequately formulated for the police. Nonetheless, social workers' (and other professionals') reluctance to call on these powers is understandable because if the anxieties do not prove well-founded, there are likely to be serious repercussions in work with parents.

The second possibility is the use of the Child Assessment Order (Section 43, Children Act 1989). It is clear that this provision has not proved effective. It is 'designed to cover those situations when there are concerns about a child and lack of cooperation from the child's carers is preventing full assessment. The order is not intended to be used in obvious emergency situations' (Brammer, 2007). It does not authorise removal of a child, unless it is obviously necessary. It lasts for only seven days – a very short time for this purpose. Dickens (1993) and Lavery (1996) both suggest that it is not fit for purpose. Lavery concludes:

> 'The CAO, unlike most of the key provisions of the Act, was not the result of a detailed reflection and review of the existing law . . . It is clear that there is no satisfactory alternative way in which the court can oversee an initial assessment which is thorough enough to uncover whether a further protection order is needed, and at the same time respects the rights of both parent and child . . . The form of the current child assessment order needs to be rethought'. (Lavery, 1996, p. 56)

It is urgent that further consideration at local and national levels should be given to provisions for access to children for assessment, in order to address the key dilemma – how to remove some children early enough to prevent irreversible damage. However, and most important of all, there is a need for radical, fresh thinking about better ways of changing the behaviour of parents and safeguarding the child.

Over the years, there have been attempts to assess and intervene in such cases by the placement of the whole family in a residential setting for limited periods of time. Such a setting affords unique opportunities for observation of family interaction and a safer place for assessment of risk to take place. Moreover, it is a setting in which a good deal of practical support and therapeutic help can be offered. However, such centres are extremely costly and arguably cannot give a realistic picture of the risk to children in such protected circumstances. More controversially, it has proved in the past more difficult to avoid excessive identification with the vulnerable, needy parents most likely to be compliant within that setting (Lynch & Stevenson, 1990).

Modes of intervention

Many professionals are familiar with the medical model of prevention: primary, secondary and tertiary. Gough (1993) sums up the three levels, as constructed in medicine, as:

(1)   Primary: interventions aimed at 'whole' populations.
(2)   Secondary: interventions aimed at individuals or groups considered to be at risk.
(3)   Tertiary: reactive interventions concerned to prevent unwanted events recurring.

Whilst there are difficulties and tensions in transferring such a model to the field of social welfare (Parton, 1985; Gough, 1993), it remains a useful way of distinguishing different kinds of activity within this field.

The main focus of this chapter is upon that level of intervention which might be described as tertiary. Our emphasis throughout has been on serious neglect, which places the children in serious jeopardy. Common sense suggests, of course, that earlier identification and intervention ('secondary intervention') is highly desirable; such cases are on a continuum rather than clearly distinguished. Thus, much of the discussion which follows is applicable to a range of cases which fall at different points on the continuum. Indeed, it would be understandable and in line with present thinking if some neglectful families were to be supported as 'in need' rather than requiring child protection procedures. However, it is not an option to turn away from the gravest cases. The consequences for the children are too damaging.

The implication of the 'ecological map' presented in Chapter 1 is that intervention may be attempted of many kinds and in many ways, related to the various systems which impact on the family. This does not necessarily mean that intervention need or should address so many diverse factors in individual cases. The question to be asked is: 'what might make a difference in this case?'

The research reviews conducted by Gaudin (1993) and MacDonald (2001) demonstrate with depressing clarity how difficult it is to change the behaviour of seriously dysfunctional families in which there is child maltreatment *and* how difficult it is to construct reliable evidence bases on evaluative studies. Readers of this book who are familiar with seriously neglectful families will need no persuading of this. However, based on her review, MacDonald (2001) offers some advice, derived from research evidence, which provides a good starting point for the kind of 'tertiary prevention' appropriate for seriously neglectful families. She suggests:

- That cognitive behavioural approaches for parents of young children (for example, under ten) are some of the most helpful. ('Cognitive behavioural', derived from social learning theory, 'emphasises . . . that the acquisition of skills requires more than just insight or discussion . . . and that one of the most effective means of acquiring skills is through modelling'.) (p. 154).
- That the families, sometimes described as 'chaotic' and 'multi-problem', will require a range of interventions of which cognitive behavioural is only one (p. 173).
- That long-standing complex problems may well require long-term as well as shorter-term intensive patterns of intervention (p. 173).
- The establishing of trust between worker and family takes time but is critical to success (p. 173).
- That cognitive behavioural approaches are especially useful in working with parents with learning disabilities (p. 175).

These observations, derived from evaluative studies, focus upon work with parent(s). They have to be balanced with precise plans for complementary care for the children, which I shall discuss in detail later. This is fundamental to any strategy for keeping the family intact. However, such care plans imply that there is some degree of acceptance by the parent(s), otherwise they are bound to fail. The agreement of the parent(s) to cooperate must be tested by their actions, not just their words. A critical aspect of assessment will be an evaluation of the attitudes of parent(s) to their current situation and to 'authority' in the shape of child protection services. It is unsurprising that parent(s) may be hostile to workers whom they see as holding so much power over their lives. Indeed, it has been suggested that it might be preferable for ongoing work to be undertaken by different workers to those who have been involved in the assessment and/or court processes. Whilst there may be specific circumstances in which such a division is desirable, issues of trust between workers and parent(s), of workers' reliability and honesty, and their capacity to experience and to demonstrate empathy are fundamental to such relationships. This is one crucial reason for longer-term interventions than are at present usual. It adds weight to the case for 'core teams' outlined in the previous chapter.

If assessment is done well (and it is accepted that this is as yet highly variable), there will be some families in which the non-compliance of the parent(s), for whatever reason, and the harm being done to the children, rules out the challenging and lengthy process of holding the family together. If, however, there is to be a systematic attempt to keep the family together, the worker must be prepared for 'confused ambivalence' in the parents which may result in actions which jeopardise care plans.

Indeed, there is a welter of feelings aroused in parent(s) and children, as well as in the 'complementary carers', whether volunteers, quasi-foster parents, relatives or the workers themselves. If these are not dealt with, they can result in a spiral of negativity which is damaging to the children. (Such situations can mirror the experiences which children have within their own families, when adults fall out.) The work which is required in holding things together involves empathy and sensitivity of a high order, which should be supported by reflective supervision/consultation. The worker has to 'tune in' to the meaning and behaviour of the different parties. Some will point out that work of this quality is in short supply. In my view, 'managing ambivalence' to avoid destructive outcomes is integral to good practice generally; the dynamics when care of children is involved are particularly explosive.

Help for parents 'as people'

Earlier chapters have highlighted a number of problems commonly found in parents of seriously neglected children. These include low self-esteem, social isolation, dysfunctional relationships with the wider family, and acute and chronic poverty as a backdrop to much else. It follows that the parents themselves have needs which affect the care of their children but which exist independently of the children. To attend to those needs may play a part in improving the parents' ability and willingness to attend to their children's needs.

In the discussion of gender (Chapter 3), it was suggested that for some women, motherhood was not welcomed. It was pointed out that those in more favourable material and financial circumstances can buy their way out of total immersion in the mothering role. Government policy in recent years has laid much emphasis on employment and less dependence on benefits as beneficial to the individual woman and to society. There is, of course, much debate about the practicability and desirability of such policies. Debate about the former, practicability, turns upon issues of child care, costs and job availability; the latter, much less openly, centres upon the effect on young children and the attachment processes of splitting adult care.

However, if, as is the case with the families we are discussing, there are serious deficits in the care children are receiving at home, the objections to such child care arrangements are obviously weakened. But obstacles to women's employment may reflect the reality of the local situation, with financial advantages and disadvantages for a particular woman. It is also highly probable that for some such women the psychological and social journey from where they are now to the world of work will be a long and difficult one. They may need help with literacy, numeracy, IT skills, personal organisation and many other issues before employment prospects are realistic. The central argument, nonetheless, is a powerful one. Put briefly, it is that women who feel they are failures and that no one minds about them may need to be offered something for *themselves* before they can be better mothers. It is likely that well-supported, practical plans, underpinned by reliable workers, will offer the best chances of raising self-esteem.

These ideas are, of course, well established in policies for women generally. The challenge (and it is formidable) is to see whether, slowly but steadily, some of the mothers who are currently seen to be at the bottom of the ladder can be helped to climb up out of the pervasive fog of failure which at present surrounds them. Opportunities, for example in relation to literacy or 'using a PC' will present themselves. But to take them up requires a degree of self-confidence and help with practical arrangements. The availability of a worker to help in this may make the difference between success or failure in the early stages of a plan for the woman's personal development. This involves a shift of thinking from 'child-centred' to 'woman-centred'. The central purpose of safeguarding a seriously neglected child must be kept clear – there is always a danger of losing focus. It may, therefore, be necessary that for this purpose a different worker should be involved.

The position of fathers in relation to this group of families was discussed in Chapter 3; relatively few of these families will have a father in long-term residence. However, when there is, the issue of balancing support for the fathering role with support for the needs of the man for a wider role in society which gives him self-respect, and which is not associated with criminally destructive activities (in the world of drugs, for example), merits equally serious consideration.

Unfortunately, there are not tailor-made professionals with the skills to help the men or women who have these needs, although in some cases adult mental health services, or those for men and women with learning disabilities, could have an important part to play. In the meanwhile, if some women are helped to a greater degree of self-reliance, they will be less prone to the destructive interactions with men including domestic violence, which are, at present, so common.

The wider family

Chapter 2 explored at some length the relationships of parents with wider family members. The evidence suggests that these are frequently unsatisfactory or actively dysfunctional and it is unfortunately unlikely that the wider family can be mobilised to offer practical or emotional support beyond what is already available. Furthermore, there may be dark areas, for example of abuse, when parents were children, which are contraindications to working more closely with the wider family. Thus, caution needs to be exercised in opening up these contacts; there needs also to be an awareness that supportive offers of help may not be sustained. Nonetheless, despite these caveats, the importance of taking these relationships seriously, whether in terms of their current impact or their past, internalised, effects on parents, must be emphasised. One way or other, they affect the status quo. This has implications for case management. For example, in relation to attachment, who has parented the parents and how? How does this impact on the present situation? There is also an important proviso. Research evidence seeks for generalisations; whilst it may be broadly true that we should not expect the wider family in these cases to provide substantial help, there will be exceptions. There may be individuals whose willingness to be involved has not been understood. For example, there may be a sister or an aunt who has remained, for a variety of reasons, at the periphery of the family but who has deep feelings of concern about the current situation. This is one of the possible outcomes of the Family Group Conference model, discussed earlier.

However, it is important that such arrangements are facilitated by a social worker and the contributions made are carefully defined. Experience in other fields, such as community care of elderly people, suggests that people are anxious about taking on too much responsibility, especially when there are concerns about risk – whether to children or adults. While the objective of family group conferences may usually be to empower the wider family to look after its own, there needs to be a keen awareness of the complexities and risks when other relatives are drawn into the lives of some neglectful families.

The neighbourhood and wider community

We are familiar with the angry responses which the behaviour of these families elicits from those in the neighbourhood and of neighbours' reluctance to become involved in child protection. (Anonymous phone calls to social services reflect the anxiety, uncertainty and anger such families may provoke.) We face an intractable problem when the behaviour of each to the other escalates to an intolerable degree, or when the isolated family turns on those who have rejected them. There are issues here for youth and community workers, whose role has been little discussed in recent years, in relation to the work of children's services, which have remained largely 'case based' and individualistic in their ways of working. The families discussed here are often the most threatening to the equilibrium of the neighbourhood and therefore there may sometimes be no alternative to 'moving them on'. The importance of including, in this fresh start, the dimension of community relations cannot be overemphasised. Social exclusion is a painful and destructive aspect of the lives of these parents and children; life in a neighbourhood is one important element of this.

The concept of 'shared care'

Plans for 'shared care' can only be made when it has been decided that the deficits in parenting are not so overwhelming as to outweigh the value of the ties between parents and children. Complementary care introduces into the care plan a formal recognition that a particular child's needs at a particular time cannot be met by the parent(s) but that there may be others who can meet those needs.

The social worker is pivotal in such plans; this may well involve a long-term commitment by children's services and the social worker must accept a role 'in managing dependency' (Tanner & Turney, 2003). As earlier discussed, success or failure of complementary care plans will turn, in large degree, on the extent to which they are accepted by the parent(s).

The continuum of complementary care

This can be categorised as follows:

- Home-based care, play, activity and using volunteers or children's centre workers.
- Daily care for preschool children at nurseries, preschool provision, children's centres or daily 'foster homes'.
- For school-aged children, some provision of daily care outside ordinary school hours, possibly school based, or in a daily 'foster home'.
- For children of all ages, although less desirable for very young children, a range of planned, regular breaks away from home. (This is the equivalent to 'respite care', a term which in my view should be replaced.)
- Older children may spend part of the week, or month or year with another family, in residential schools or other facilities.

Home-based care, play or activity

This is familiar territory; much Sure Start work is based on this level of activity. It offers an opportunity for both parent(s) and children to be helped together. This is not simply about helping and supporting parents, although this objective may also have a high priority. It may also be used as a model by which parent(s) can see alternative ways of caring and coping. The national Home Start agency offers a prominent example of such work which has been increasingly used by statutory authorities in the development of preventative work, including those who have been identified as having children at some degree of risk from parenting difficulties.

Home Start is a voluntary organisation, staffed by volunteers who offer regular support, friendship and practical help to young families under stress in their own homes, helping to prevent crisis and break-down. Evaluative research (Frost *et al.*, 1997) strongly confirms the value of the Home Start model as seen by the professional 'referrers', usually health visitors and social workers, and by the users, parents and children.

In the past few years Home Start has grown significantly. In 2004 it was awarded a grant of more than £5 million (over two years) to set up schemes in every town, city and county district in England (Home Start, 2004). There has also been expansion in other parts of the UK. Home Start makes a bold claim: 'to offer every family who asks for support an individual service, tailored to their needs, at the level and frequency that is right for them'. More than 30 000 families were helped in 2005, of whom more than two-thirds were supported in their own homes by a trained volunteer (others were helped in other ways, for example in groups) (Home Start, 2005). However, it is important to note that, in 2004, of the 64 000 children supported by Home Start, only about 2000 were on the Child Protection Registers: that is around 3%.

The children who are the focus of this book are likely to be on the register, or whatever 'list' replaces it. There is a difficult issue behind these facts. Is it possible to utilise the model in relation to families when parents are, at the least, ambivalent about receiving help and who will be aware, and may be afraid, of social services' concern about them? Furthermore, can this valuable 'volunteeristic' approach to work with families be maintained alongside the necessary protective and safe-guarding processes? These matters have been a long-standing source of debate and uncertainty within Home Start; children on the register for current neglect may pose particular problems for the volunteers, whose commitment to supporting parents is central to their mission and who may experience conflict about 'telling tales'.

It remains to be seen whether the admirable objectives and achievements of organisations such as Home Start can be used as a basis for this work, finely balanced between surveillance and support. This raises an important question about the part which may be played by those outside the statutory framework of public services, for Home

Start stands between the informal and the formal; its structures are formalised but its mission is to offer good, caring neighbours, with some additional training. Such agencies can offer the structure and protection to individual 'helpers' who, as we shall discuss, are extremely difficult to find for neglectful families. There are, of course, well-established national charities, such as Barnados and the Children's Society, who are also offering services and who have a tradition of 'professionalised' help as well as that of volunteers.

Care through nursery/preschool provision

Every Child Matters (DfES, 2004) launched a major new initiative, indicated by the change of terminology from 'family centres' to 'children's centres', for the development of more comprehensive and integrated services. As an instrument of government policy, children's centres are aimed at a much wider population than the children who are the focus of this book. The key question is whether they will prove hospitable or inhospitable to those children and their families who are often ostracised and stigmatised by others. There are long-standing and familiar problems here, which resonate with debates about special or 'ordinary' schools. Children's centres as a universal resource for all children chime with the objective of social inclusion, but unless there is special thought given to those who are in, or are in the margins of, social exclusion, it is easy to see how these 'difficult' families may be squeezed out. There will be a need to 'reach out' in many practical ways and to avoid situations in which 'difference' is too hard for the children and their families to bear and in which they are actually unwelcome.

Tunstill *et al.* (2007) in their exploration of the 'tensions and opportunities between family centres and social services' highlight how difficult a challenge it will be to balance 'universalist' and 'specialist' objectives in the centres. The relationships between family centre workers and social workers in child protection were often quite fraught:

> 'It was impossible to ignore the enduring nature of the tension for both agencies to balance prevention and protection at the overall social services level. For example, the balance between early and late intervention family support services could represent a major source of tension between family centres and mainstream social services.' (Tunstill *et al.*, 2007, p. 69)

The authors argue that, given many of the most disadvantaged and problematic parents will not be in employment:

> 'The Government's long-standing emphasis on return to work as a way out of poverty . . . combined with the extension of the

catchment areas in which parents are entitled to access daycare, is highly likely to push the socio-economic characteristics of parents using the centres towards the more affluent.' (Tunstill *et al.*, 2007, p. 140)

They suggest that there is already evidence to support this. It will need skilled and imaginative management to ensure that this promising initiative does not compound the social isolation of these neglected children and their parents by rejecting them.

Extended or 'wrap-around' schools

For older children, similar issues arise to those in children's centres. There are many possibilities for 'complementary care'; we know of breakfasts provided within the school context; activities after the school day need not be specifically tied to requirements of parents who are working. Provision turns on the political will at national and local levels to include these neglected children. It is clearly preferable for them to be helped within their peer group, but for some their behavioural and emotional needs will have to be met by more individualised attention, such as 'having tea' with someone who may best be described as a 'daily foster parent' (not 'a minder') some days of the week.

There is a strong case for developing a community resource called foster parents, aunties, uncles, grannies and granddads, or call it what you will, who can offer a range of flexible care for some needy children. This can be envisaged on a continuum from regular meetings during the day within the locality to more extended arrangements, such as weekday or weekend overnight stays. This would be determined by the particular situation of the family and the needs of the children. Thus, for example, for a young school-aged child, a weekday or weekend meeting might be linked to practice at reading (but with a nice tea included). For a slightly older child, there might be longer periods in which there were certain targets for behavioural improvement, for example of self-control. Behind specific objectives there would lie the intention to offer a reliable and nurturing relationship. In recent years, there has been increased interest in 'inter-generational' relationships between children and older people. There have been some important initiatives, both in the USA and the UK (for example *Journal of Intergenerational Relations* 2003). The demographic trends and the growing numbers of fit 'young elderly' may offer an opportunity for this form of 'social volunteering' (provided expenses are generous) which could be of inestimable value. This is not a pipe dream but it would require skilled professional management.

The model of fostering which has been described as 'respite care' (it is time to find another phrase) is better known, but has usually been applied to help for families with a child who is disabled. There is little indication that the work described by Aldgate *et al.* (1996) as offering 'respite' care to a wider range of families under stress has developed much in the past decade. It is evident from the description of these families that a good many of their characteristics were those which we have seen in neglectful parents. However, it may well be that the intensity of some difficulties and some additional problems, particular to such parents, would further complicate the task of arranging and managing short-term placements for such families. The children's need for them, however, may be equally, or more, pressing.

Aldgate *et al.* outline the purposes for which respite care is appropriate:

- 'To provide relief from the normal stresses of being a parent.
- To provide children with relief from stressful family living.
- To help manage children's behaviour.
- To provide a link with the community for families living in social isolation.
- To help with relief from the stress of living in continuing poverty.
- To offer an alternative to admission to full-time accommodation.
- To provide a relief for sick parents.
- To provide an early diversion from potential physical abuse.
- To build parents' self-esteem.
- To offer a different and relaxing experience for children.' (Aldgate *et al.*, 1996, p. 151)

Many of the opportunities which this list suggests are obviously relevant to the support of neglected children as well as to their parents. Indeed, one might develop and expand the possible gains to neglected children, as individuals, of reliable periods of 'good enough' care, in all aspects of their development, not least the physical.

The results of the placements studied by Aldgate *et al.* are highly relevant to our theme. For example, parental self-esteem improved and over half the parents began to address their social isolation. The emphasis of the service was on providing a family placement that did not threaten parental responsibility. The children who were observed and talked to were between 1 and 15 years. They were 'usually quite clear what the arrangements were and why they had been made' and were very positive about the experience.

In my opinion, this form of complementary care should form a crucial element in the care packages for 'our' neglected children.

Older children living away for periods of time

This opens up an area which has been very little explored. It goes beyond the notion of 'respite care' to an acceptance that for some older children, this may be the only way to ensure they can sustain links with their parents, and not be irretrievably harmed by them. There are a number of variations on this theme. The first is a foster placement. Such plans could, of course, include placements with relatives. The subject of 'kinship care' has not been adequately integrated into child care policy and practice and considered analysis is long overdue. Government interest is mounting, however, and the recent publication *Assessment in Kinship Care* (Talbot & Calder, 2006) is welcome. Kinship care of children in the case of parents with learning disabilities is common and it may well be that there are many informal arrangements whereby children are in fact spending their lives between the parents and other relatives, in forms of shared care which do not involve social services. But when serious neglect is involved, formal involvement will be inevitable. These complex issues are usefully explored by Young (Young, 2006).

In other kinds of seriously 'neglectful' parents, when cognitive limitation is not the issue, accessible and suitable relatives are much less likely to be available. The problematic nature of these arrangements is discussed by Freeman and Ingham (Freeman & Ingham, 2006). It is not surprising, but sobering, to read of the interconnected families with patterns of multiple abuse, in which some neglectful parents are embedded. It is, therefore, more likely that alternative families will be found outside the kinship network. Even so, this is likely to require very special gifts and attitudes; aspects of this are discussed later.

There remain other possibilities. The present position regarding the provision of residential care within local authorities is far from satisfactory. There are a number of contraindications for such placements: the shortage of places, the highly disturbed, delinquent and largely adolescent population of these homes, and the fact that they often do not provide a warm and nurturing environment do not make them likely 'refuges' for a group of neglected children, a number of whom will be between the ages of (for example) 8 and 12 years.

It is possible to envisage a form of boarding school provision, weekly or termly, for children whose home care falls short of 'good enough', which would address not only educational needs, although these are often of great significance, but which would also be structured and planned in such a way as to offer experiences of comfort, warmth and stability to compensate for what is lacking at home. Into such an environment, seriously neglected children might live with others whose social circumstances gave rise to similar needs. The traditional idea of a bleak 'boarding schools' for younger children is outmoded, as many parents of privileged children know from their own experience.

Conclusion

A powerful case can be made, both moral and practical, for paying close attention to the needs and problems of families in which children are seriously neglected. There are five key issues:

- How far, and in what ways, can the capacity of parents to change their behaviour towards their children be improved?
- What are the implications of this for the assessment process?
- How can the present disjunction between 'system delays' and children's developmental needs be minimised?
- Success in intervention is critically dependent on the capacity of workers to establish a relationship of trust and (at least to some extent) cooperation between parents and workers. (When this is missing, the outlook is bleak.)
- There is a need for radical, flexible thinking about 'a continuum of shared care' for the children, in which deficits in parental care are, to an extent, made good by others.

In essence, the argument of this book has been that stark choices face agencies, especially children's services, if this issue is to be treated with the seriousness it deserves. Children must not be left in developmental limbo: this requires radical changes both within the local authority and in judicial processes. Either children must be removed at an age early enough to make their chances of a successful alternative life realistic, or they must be provided with complementary care. The latter is likely to involve arrangements over a long time and is dependent on parental cooperation. The skills of the social workers in facilitating this are critical to success. All this requires a political, judicial and professional will to examine all aspects of current policies and practices which at present impact negatively upon seriously neglected children. Workers at the level of practice, from a wide range of agencies and professions, cannot achieve the necessary improvements alone, although their commitment is indispensable. Do we care enough?

Appendices

Introduction to appendices

These appendices are intended to deepen awareness of the functioning of a particular family. I have been very conscious that many workers feel overloaded with forms and lists. These appendices are intended to be helpful, especially if they are used in discussion with others, when assessing the extent and nature of the harm which the children may be suffering in neglectful families. It is understood that they will have to be used as professional 'aide memoire', alongside more formal assessment procedures. The third checklist on attachment (p. 150) was prepared to help foster or adoptive parents but it is also very helpful for the understanding of attachment generally.

Appendices

Appendix I

Parent–Child Interactions

Visit No: Assessor: Name of client:

	often	*seldom*	*almost never*
Child's reactive and proactive behaviour:			
(1) Playing family			
(2) Laughing/smiling			
(3) Running			
(4) Talking freely			
(5) Coming for help			
(6) Coming for comfort			
(7) Cuddling up to parents			
(8) Responding to affection			
(9) Responding to attention			
(10) At ease when parents are near			
(11) Joining in activities with other children			
(12) Not frightened when approached by parents or corrected			
Father's/mother's reactive and proactive behaviour:	*often*	*seldom*	*almost never*
(1) Talking to the child			
(2) Looking at the child			
(3) Smiling at the child			
(4) Making eye contact (lovingly)			
(5) Touching (gently)			
(6) Holding (closely, lovingly)			
(7) Playing			
(8) Cuddling			
(9) Kissing			

	often	seldom	almost never
(10) Sitting the child on the lap			
(11) Handling the child in a gentle way			
(12) Giving requests (as opposed to commands)			
(13) Helping the child if it is in difficulties			
(14) Encouraging the child when it cries or when it is hurt			
(15) Being concerned about the child			
(16) Picking the child up when it cries or when it is hurt			
(17) Answering the child's questions			
(18) Not ignoring the child's presence			
(19) Emotionally treating the child the same as other children			
(20) Handling the children consistently			
Siblings' reactive and proactive behaviour:			
(1) Playing with the child			
(2) Talking to the child			
(3) Participating in activities			
(4) Accepting the child			
(5) Treating the child well			
(6) Pushing the child away and rejecting it			
(7) Blaming the child for everything that happens			
(8) Protecting the child			
(9) Helping the child when in difficulties or in trouble			
(10) Scapegoating the child			

Quality of Care

Assessment of physical and emotional neglect: quality of child care at home

Physical care of the child

(1) Is the child appropriately dressed for the weather?
(2) Is the child's clothing appropriate?
(3) Is the child's clothing regularly changed?
(4) Is the child washed and bathed?
(5) Is hygiene at home reasonable?
(6) Is a cot/pram/bed available?
(7) Are sleeping arrangements appropriate?
(8) Is the room warm?
(9) Is safety observed, such as fire, electric points, sharp objects, medicine, chemical substances, etc.?
(10) Are supervision and guidance provided for the child?
(11) Is medical attention provided when the child is not well?

Nutrition

The questions below may help to assess non-organic failure to thrive and nutritional neglect. Failure to thrive assessment should also include parent–child interaction during the process of feeding and other child care activities.

(1) Is the child regularly fed?
(2) Is the child given enough food?

(3) Is the child given appropriate food?
(4) Is the child handled patiently during feeding/eating?
(5) Is the child encouraged to eat?
(6) Is there reasonable flexibility in feeding/eating routine?
(7) Is there evidence of anger, frustration and force feeding during the feeding/eating period?
(8) Is the child punished for not eating?
(9) Is there awareness that the child is too thin?
(10) Is there concern about the child's well-being?
(11) Is there evidence of seeking help and advice?
(12) Is there evidence of responding to help and advice?

From Iwaniec, D. (1995) *The Emotionally Abused and Neglected Child* (p. 92). John Wiley, Chichester.

Appendix III

Attachment

Attachment

(1) Birth to 1 year

Does the child:

- Appear alert?
- Respond to humans?
- Show interest in the human face?
- Track with his/her eyes?
- Vocalise frequently?
- Exhibit expected motor development?
- Enjoy close physical contact?
- Exhibit discomfort?
- Appear to be easily comforted?
- Exhibit normal or excessive fussiness?
- Appear outgoing or is he/she passive and withdrawn?
- Have good muscle tone?
- Other.

Does the parent(s):

- Respond to the infant's vocalisations?
- Change tone in voice when talking to the infant or about the infant?
- Show interest in face-to-face contact with the infant?
- Exhibit interest in and encourage age appropriate development?

- Respond to the child's indications of discomfort?
- Show the ability to comfort the child?
- Enjoy close physical contact with the child?
- Initiate positive interactions with the child?
- Identify positive or negative qualities in the child that remind the parent of another family member?
- Other.

(2) 1 to 5 years

Does the child:

- Explore the environment in a normal way?
- Respond to parent(s)?
- Keep themself occupied in a positive way?
- Seem relaxed and happy?
- Have the ability to express emotions?
- React to pain and pleasure?
- Engage in age appropriate activity?
- Use speech appropriately?
- Express frustration?
- Respond to parental limit setting?
- Exhibit observable fears?
- React positively to physical closeness?
- Respond appropriately to separation from parent?
- Respond appropriately to parent's return?
- Exhibit body rigidity or relaxation?
- Other.

(3) Primary schoolchildren

Does the child:

- Behave as though they like themself?
- Appear proud of accomplishments?
- Share?
- Perform well academically?
- Always test limits?
- Try new tasks?
- React realistically to making a mistake? Does he/she show fear, anger or acceptance?
- Have the ability to express emotions?
- Establish eye contact?
- Exhibit confidence in their abilities or do they frequently say 'I don't know'?
- Appear to be developing a conscience?
- Move in a relaxed way or is the body rigid?
- Feel comfortable speaking to adults?

- Smile easily?
- React to parent(s) being physically close?
- Have positive interactions with siblings and/or peers?
- Appear comfortable with his/her sexual identifications?
- Other.

Does the parent:

- Show interest in the child's school performance?
- Accept expression of negative feelings?
- Respond to child's overtures?
- Give support for the child in terms of developing healthy peer relationships?
- Handle problems between siblings equitably?
- Initiate affectionate disciplinary measures?
- Assign age appropriate responsibilities to the child?
- Other.

(4) Adolescents

Is the adolescent:

- Aware of his/her strong points?
- Aware of his/her weak points?
- Comfortable with his/her sexuality?
- Engaging in positive peer interactions?
- Performing satisfactorily in school?
- Exhibiting signs of conscience development?
- Free from severe problems with the law?
- Accepting and/or rejecting his/her parents' value system?
- Keeping themself occupied in appropriate ways?
- Comfortable with reasonable limits or is he/she constantly involved in control issues?
- Developing interests outside the home?
- Other.

Does the parent(s):

- Set appropriate limits?
- Encourage appropriate autonomy?
- Trust the adolescent?
- Show interest in and acceptance of the adolescent's friends?
- Display interest in the adolescent's school performance?
- Exhibit interest in the adolescent's outside activities?
- Have reasonable expectations of chores and/or responsibilities adolescents should assume?
- Stand by the adolescent if he/she gets into trouble?
- Show affection?

- Think this child will 'turn out okay'?
- Other.

Checklist: ways to encourage attachment

Responding to the arousal/relaxation cycle

- Using the child's tantrums to encourage attachment.
- Responding to the child when he/she is physically ill.
- Accompanying the child to doctor and dentist appointments.
- Helping the child express and cope with feelings of anger and frustration.
- Sharing the child's extreme excitement over his/her achievements.
- Helping the child cope with feelings about moving.
- Helping the child cope with ambivalent feelings about his/her birth family.
- Helping the child learn more about his/her past.
- Responding to a child who is hurt or injured.
- Educating the child about sexual issues.
- Other.

Initiating positive interactions

- Making affectionate overtures: hugs, kisses, physical closeness.
- Reading to the child.
- Sharing the child's 'life book'.
- Playing games.
- Going shopping together for clothes/toys for the child.
- Going on special outings: circus, plays or the like.
- Supporting the child's outside activities by providing transport or being a group leader.
- Helping the child with homework when he or she needs it.
- Teaching the child to cook or bake.
- Saying 'I love you'.
- Teaching the child about extended family members through pictures and talk.
- Helping the child understand the family 'jokes' or sayings.
- Teaching the child to participate in family activities such as bowling, camping or skiing.
- Helping the child meet the expectations of the other parent.
- Other.

Encouraging behaviour

- Encouraging the child to practise calling parents 'mum' and 'dad'.
- Adding a middle name to incorporate a name of family significance.
- Hanging pictures of a child on a wall.
- Involving the child in family reunions and similar activities.
- Involving the child in grandparent visits.
- Involving the child in family rituals.
- Holding religious ceremonies or other ceremonies that incorporate the child in the family.
- Buying new clothes for the child as a way of becoming acquainted with the child's size, colour preferences, style preferences and the like.
- Making statements such as 'in our family we do it this way' in supportive fashion.
- Sending out announcements of adoption.

Vera Fahlberg first developed this series of checklists. Reproduced with kind permission from the British Association for Adoption and Fostering, *Good Enough Parenting: A Framework for Assessment* p. 91 by M. Adcock and R. White.

Appendix IV

Neglected Children

The attached form will take about ten minutes to complete. It was designed to help assess the risk to children under the age of seven years from the effects of neglectful parenting. It was anticipated that the form would be completed once an initial assessment had been completed in relation to 'neglect' referrals. The form is to be completed by the key worker and would be completed every time the case was reviewed. By doing this, it is hoped that a more objective measure could be achieved in relation to 'good enough parenting standards' in such cases.

Experience is showing that if the form is completed after initial investigations any gaps in the investigating worker's knowledge of the family become readily apparent. While the form was designed to assess risk to younger children, it can still be used in relation to older children.

The higher the score, the higher the element of neglect in the family.

It is taken from Minty and Pattinson (1994). This is a revised, as yet untested risk assessment for neglected children, building on work reported in the *British Journal of Social Work* (1994). It stands the test of time well and is reproduced with kind permission of the author. It may be used in conjunction with the Home Conditions Assessment. (Cox & Bentovim, DoH, 2000c)

Scale for Assessing Neglectful Parenting

Case No: _____

Family name(s): _____

Family composition: _____
(note ages and sex of children)

Family involved in neglect project: Yes/No

Date completed: _____

Completed by: _____

0 = Definitely untrue or never true

1 = Partially true or occasionally true

2 = Largely true or often true

3 = Definitely true or always true

NK = Not known

A   Food and eating habits

(1)   There is insufficient food in the house to meet the children's
        needs for the next 12 hours. | 0 | 1 | 2 | 3 | NK |

(2)   Babies and toddlers are given food which is inappropriate for
        their age. | 0 | 1 | 2 | 3 | NK |

(3)   There are inadequate working facilities which permit meals to be
        prepared (e.g. cooker/stove). | 0 | 1 | 2 | 3 | NK |

(4)   There is inadequate cooking equipment (e.g. pots and pans).
                                                          | 0 | 1 | 2 | 3 | NK |

(5)   The nutritional content of meals does not appear to be adequate.
                                                          | 0 | 1 | 2 | 3 | NK |

(6)   Children do not have even one prepared meal per day (including
        school meals). | 0 | 1 | 2 | 3 | NK |

(7)   Feeding methods for young children and babies appear to be
        unhygienic (e.g. unsatisfactory/dirty bottles). | 0 | 1 | 2 | 3 | NK |

(8)   There is no use of fresh vegetables or fruit. | 0 | 1 | 2 | 3 | NK |

(9)   There is excessive use of sugar/sweets/crisps/chips.
                                                          | 0 | 1 | 2 | 3 | NK |

(10)   There is inadequate seating for children/toddlers to have meals
        at the table. | 0 | 1 | 2 | 3 | NK |

(11)   Parents appear to feed babies without holding them.
                                                          | 0 | 1 | 2 | 3 | NK |

(12)   Children have been observed to eat excessively/ravenously.
                                                          | 0 | 1 | 2 | 3 | NK |

(13)   Children have been reported to eat excessively/ravenously.
                                                          | 0 | 1 | 2 | 3 | NK |

(14)   Children appear to be extremely hungry. | 0 | 1 | 2 | 3 | NK |

(15)   Children are reported as extremely hungry. | 0 | 1 | 2 | 3 | NK |

B   Health and hygiene

(16)   The children look dirty. | 0 | 1 | 2 | 3 | NK |

(17)   The parents look dirty. | 0 | 1 | 2 | 3 | NK |

(18)   The home lacks showering/bathing facilities which work and are
        available for washing. | 0 | 1 | 2 | 3 | NK |

(19) The bath and basin are dirty. `0 1 2 3 NK`

(20) The family lacks a toilet which works. `0 1 2 3 NK`

(21) The lavatories and toilets are dirty. `0 1 2 3 NK`

(22) The kitchen is dirty. `0 1 2 3 NK`

(23) The kitchen equipment is unwashed. `0 1 2 3 NK`

(24) Children regularly sleep in the same bed as parents. `0 1 2 3 NK`

(25) Is there a place for keeping children's clothes together (e.g. cupboard/drawers/basket/bag)? `0 1 2 3 NK`

(26) Conditions in the parents' bedroom are much superior to those in the children's bedrooms. `0 1 2 3 NK`

(27) Scraps of food are left on the living room/dining room floor. `0 1 2 3 NK`

(28) Family members suffer from headlice infections. `0 1 2 3 NK`

(29) Family members have chronic scabies. `0 1 2 3 NK`

(30) There is evidence of nappy rash that is not being treated. `0 1 2 3 NK`

(31) Children who soil/wet are left in dirty/wet clothing or a dirty/wet bed. `0 1 2 3 NK`

(32) Parents have failed to report medical problems in their children (e.g. running ears, squints, recurring diarrhoea). `0 1 2 3 NK`

(33) Parents appear to be unaware the child has a need for dental treatment. `0 1 2 3 NK`

(34) The house has a bad smell. `0 1 2 3 NK`

(35) The furniture is damp. `0 1 2 3 NK`

(36) The garden is full of dangerous rubbish. `0 1 2 3 NK`

C   *Warmth/clothing*

(37) The family lacks a heating system which works. `0 1 2 3 NK`

(38) The outside doors are badly fitted/do not work. `0 1 2 3 NK`

(39) Inside doors are left unfitted and damaged. `0 1 2 3 NK`

(40) Windows have been left unglazed/uncovered. `0 1 2 3 NK`

(41)   There is no covering on the floor.   0 | 1 | 2 | 3 | NK

(42)   The children have no adequate bedding (i.e. mattress and sheets, enough blankets or duvets).   0 | 1 | 2 | 3 | NK

(43)   The children do not have clothes appropriate for the weather.   0 | 1 | 2 | 3 | NK

(44)   The children have no waterproof coats.   0 | 1 | 2 | 3 | NK

(45)   The children's shoes let in water.   0 | 1 | 2 | 3 | NK

(46)   Children lack at least one set of a clean change of clothes.   0 | 1 | 2 | 3 | NK

(47)   The children sleep in their day clothes.   0 | 1 | 2 | 3 | NK

(48)   The bedroom window lacks curtains/blinds.   0 | 1 | 2 | 3 | NK

(49)   The curtains are left closed all day.   0 | 1 | 2 | 3 | NK

(50)   The children have clothes that do not fit them.   0 | 1 | 2 | 3 | NK

(51)   There are insufficient nappies for all babies and toddlers who need them.   0 | 1 | 2 | 3 | NK

(52)   The children's clothes smell.   0 | 1 | 2 | 3 | NK

(53)   There are large holes or tears or several missing buttons/ fasteners on the children's clothes.   0 | 1 | 2 | 3 | NK

(54)   The children's clothes are really dirty.   0 | 1 | 2 | 3 | NK

(55)   The children lack their own personal clothes.   0 | 1 | 2 | 3 | NK

D   *Safety and supervision*

(56)   The children are left alone.   0 | 1 | 2 | 3 | NK

(57)   Babysitters are under 14 years of age.   0 | 1 | 2 | 3 | NK

(58)   The parents do not know the babysitters.   0 | 1 | 2 | 3 | NK

(59)   The child(ren) has been found wandering outside the house.   0 | 1 | 2 | 3 | NK

(60)   The parents do not know where young children are when they go out to play.   0 | 1 | 2 | 3 | NK

(61)   The children do not know where the parents are.   0 | 1 | 2 | 3 | NK

(62)   The parents cannot state the limits of the children's play area.   0 | 1 | 2 | 3 | NK

(63) The parents allow young children to cross busy roads on their own. `0 | 1 | 2 | 3 | NK`

(64) For toddlers under 5 there is no safety gate which is in regular use. `0 | 1 | 2 | 3 | NK`

(65) If open or electric fires are used, there is no fireguard. `0 | 1 | 2 | 3 | NK`

(66) The children have frequent accidents involving injuries. `0 | 1 | 2 | 3 | NK`

(67) Windows can easily be opened by small children. `0 | 1 | 2 | 3 | NK`

(68) Outside doors cannot be locked. `0 | 1 | 2 | 3 | NK`

(69) Children are left in unenclosed gardens/yards. `0 | 1 | 2 | 3 | NK`

(70) Dangerous substances are placed within young children's reach. `0 | 1 | 2 | 3 | NK`

(71) Children are locked out of the house. `0 | 1 | 2 | 3 | NK`

E   *Emotional neglect*

(72) Parents hardly spend any regular time with their children. `0 | 1 | 2 | 3 | NK`

(73) Parents do not play with their children. `0 | 1 | 2 | 3 | NK`

(74) There are no regular bed times for children. `0 | 1 | 2 | 3 | NK`

(75) Under 8s are still up at 10.00 PM. `0 | 1 | 2 | 3 | NK`

(76) When children are distressed parents do not comfort them. `0 | 1 | 2 | 3 | NK`

(77) The parents have very unrealistic expectations of their children's abilities. `0 | 1 | 2 | 3 | NK`

(78) The parents expect their children to look after themselves. `0 | 1 | 2 | 3 | NK`

(79) The parents are quite unable to control small children. `0 | 1 | 2 | 3 | NK`

(80) The parents respond insensitively to their children's needs. `0 | 1 | 2 | 3 | NK`

(81) The children are indiscriminately affectionate to strangers. `0 | 1 | 2 | 3 | NK`

(82)   The children do not turn appropriately to other adults.

0 | 1 | 2 | 3 | NK

(83)   The parents have at best only a dim awareness of their children and their needs.

0 | 1 | 2 | 3 | NK

(84)   The parents' response to their children's behaviour appears to be very unpredictable.

0 | 1 | 2 | 3 | NK

(85)   Parents largely leave the children to their own devices.

0 | 1 | 2 | 3 | NK

(86)   Parents are violent in front of their children.

0 | 1 | 2 | 3 | NK

(87)   Parents frequently argue in front of their children.

0 | 1 | 2 | 3 | NK

(88)   Parents frequently argue when their children are in the house, but out of sight.

0 | 1 | 2 | 3 | NK

(89)   The parents have made suicide attempts in front of their children.

0 | 1 | 2 | 3 | NK

(90)   The parents have made suicide threats in front of their children.

0 | 1 | 2 | 3 | NK

(91)   The parents have threatened to leave the children or put them into care if they do not behave.

0 | 1 | 2 | 3 | NK

(92)   Frequently no action is taken to check bad and/or dangerous behaviour.

0 | 1 | 2 | 3 | NK

(93)   Children are not encouraged to care for their toys.

0 | 1 | 2 | 3 | NK

(94)   The parents appear to set no limit to TV watching.

0 | 1 | 2 | 3 | NK

(95)   A parent fails to show pride in their child's achievement.

0 | 1 | 2 | 3 | NK

(96)   Mother/father cannot show physical affection to the child/children.

0 | 1 | 2 | 3 | NK

(97)   Children are not encouraged to paint or draw or play constructively.

0 | 1 | 2 | 3 | NK

(98)   Children have no books of their own.

0 | 1 | 2 | 3 | NK

(99)   Children have no age appropriate toys, dolls.

0 | 1 | 2 | 3 | NK

(100)   Parents do not teach their children the difference between right or wrong in a manner appropriate to their level of development.

| 0 | 1 | 2 | 3 | NK |

(101)   The parents buy themselves expensive clothes, jewels, consumer goods, but provide hardly anything for the children.

| 0 | 1 | 2 | 3 | NK |

(102)   Bullying or cruelty by older siblings to younger siblings goes unchecked.

| 0 | 1 | 2 | 3 | NK |

(103)   Children are locked in bedrooms, cupboards.

| 0 | 1 | 2 | 3 | NK |

(104)   Dangerous animals are left insufficiently controlled.

| 0 | 1 | 2 | 3 | NK |

(105)   The animals appear better fed and cared for than the children.

| 0 | 1 | 2 | 3 | NK |

(106)   Spiteful or cruel play with pets goes unchecked.

| 0 | 1 | 2 | 3 | NK |

(107)   The house or garden/yard is frequently fouled with animal faeces/urine.

| 0 | 1 | 2 | 3 | NK |

F   School

(108)   Parents regularly withdraw their children from school/nursery.

| 0 | 1 | 2 | 3 | NK |

(109)   Children regularly turn up late for school/nursery.

| 0 | 1 | 2 | 3 | NK |

(110)   School-age children are regularly not provided with an adequate lunch or dinner money.

| 0 | 1 | 2 | 3 | NK |

(111)   Infant/nursery children make their own way to school/nursery by themselves.

| 0 | 1 | 2 | 3 | NK |

Do not score this section

| YES | NO |

(a)   Parents report feeding difficulties with a child.

| | |

(b)   Feeding problems are observed in relation to a particular child.

| | |

(c)   Children have been observed to eat excessively slowly.

| | |

(d) Children have been reported to eat excessively slowly.

C1

(a) The families can afford to pay for their heating systems.

(b) There are serious structural deficiencies in the house (e.g. rotten floor boards, leaking roof).

(c) The house is unusually damp.

Appendix V

The Assessment Framework

Department of Health (2000) *Framework for the Assessment of Children in Need and their Families.* Stationery Office, London.

Murphy, H. & Harbin, F. (2003) The assessment of parental substance abuse and its impact on child care. In: *Assessment in Child Care* (eds M.C. Calder & S. Hackett), pp. 353–61. Russell House Publishing, Lyme Regis.

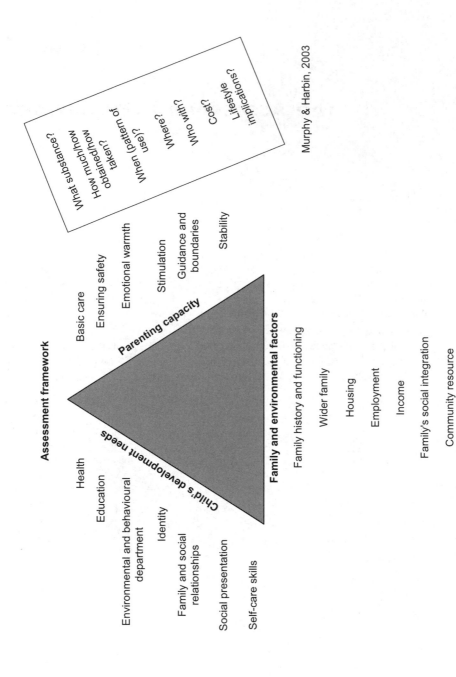

Assessment framework

Child's developmental needs

Health
Education
Environmental and behavioural department
Identity
Family and social relationships
Social presentation
Self-care skills

Parenting capacity

Basic care
Ensuring safety
Emotional warmth
Stimulation
Guidance and boundaries
Stability

Family and environmental factors

Family history and functioning
Wider family
Housing
Employment
Income
Family's social integration
Community resource

What substance?
How much/how obtained/how taken?
When (pattern of use)?
Where?
Who with?
Cost?
Lifestyle implications?

Murphy & Harbin, 2003

Department of Health, The Assessment Framework, 2000

References

Adams, P. (1999) Towards a family support. Approach with drug using parents. *Child Abuse Review*, **8** (1), 15–28.

Adcock, M. & White, R. (1985) *Good Enough Parenting: a Framework for Assessment*, p. 91. British Agencies for Adoption and Fostering, London.

Advisory Council on the Misuse of Drugs (2004) *Hidden Harm*. Home Office, London.

Aldgate, J. & Simmonds, J. (1988) *Direct Work with Children*. Batsford, London.

Aldgate, J., Bradley, M. & Hawley, D. (1996) Respite accommodation: a case study of partnership under The Children Act 1989. In: *Child Welfare Services* (eds M. Hill & J. Aldgate), pp. 147–169. Jessica Kingsley, London.

Allen, R. & Oliver, J. (1982) The effects of child maltreatment on language development. *Child Abuse and Neglect*, **6**, 299–305.

Allsopp, M. & Stevenson, O. (1995) *Social Workers' Perception of Risk in Child Protection. A Discussion Paper*. Economic and Social Research Council project, Nottingham University.

Audit Commission (2004) *Youth Justice 2004: a Review of the Reformed Youth Justice System*. Audit Commission, London.

Baird, S. & Neufeldt, D. (1988) *Assessing Potential for Abuse and Neglect*. National Council on Crime and Delinquency Focus, Washington, DC.

Bakinsky, M. (2000) *Child Protection and Education*. NSPCC, London.

Bakinsky, M. (2003) Newly Qualified Teachers in Child Protection. *Child Abuse Review*, **12**, 119–127.

Ballet Hoo (2006) Channel 4 (Autumn).

Becker, S. (1997) *Responding to Poverty*. Longman, Harrow.

Becker, S. (2003) 'Security for those who cannot': Labour's neglected welfare principle. In: *Understanding Social Security* (ed. J. Millar), pp. 104–121. The Policy Press, Bristol.

Beckhelling, J., Hartfree, Y., Legge, K. *et al.* (2006) *The Social Fund: Current Role and Future Direction*. Joseph Rowntree Foundation, York.

Birchall, E. & Hallett, C. (1995) *Working Together in Child Protection. Studies in Child Protection*. HMSO, London.

Blackburn, C. (1991) *Poverty and Health. Working with Families*. Open University Press, Buckingham.

Blair, T. (2006) *Our Nation's Future – Social Exclusion*. http://www.number10.gov. uk/output/page10037.asp

Booth, T. & Booth, W. (1993) Parenting with learning difficulties: lessons with practitioners. *British Journal of Social Work*, **23** (5), 459–80.

Booth, T. & Booth, W. (2003) Parents with learning difficulties and the stolen generation. *Journal of Learning Disabilities*, **7** (3), 203–9.

Bostock, L., Bairstow, S., Ash, S. & MacLeod, F. (2006) *Managing Risk and Minimising Mistakes in Services to Children and Families*. Social Care Institute for Excellence. The Policy Press, Bristol.

Bottoms, A. & Kemp, V. (2006) The relationship between youth justice and child welfare in England and Wales. In: *Youth Justice and Child Protection* (eds M. Hill, A. Lockyer & F. Stone), pp. 139–57. Jessica Kingsley, London.

Bowlby, J. (1973) *Attachment and Loss*, Vols 1 and 2. Hogarth Press and the Institute of Psychoanalysis, London.

Brammer, A. (2007) *Social Work Law*. Pearson Longman, Harrow.

Brent Borough Council and Brent Health Authority (1985) *Jasmine Beckford: a Child in Trust. Report of the Panel of Inquiry into the Circumstances Surrounding the Death of Jasmine Beckford*. Presented to Brent Borough Council and to Brent Health Authority.

Bronfenbrenner, U. (1979) *The Ecology of Human Development*. Harvard University Press, Cambridge, Mass.

Brown, L. (2003) Mainstream or margin? The current use of family group conferences in child welfare practice in the UK. *Child and Family Social Work*, **8** (4).

Butler-Sloss, Lord Justice (1988) *Report of the Inquiry into Child Abuse in Cleveland 1987*. HMSO, London.

Cabinet Office (2000) *Prime Minister's Review of Adoption – Issues for Consultation*. Crown Copyright, London.

Calder, M. (2004) Out of the frying pan into the fire? A critical analysis of the integrated children's system. *Child Care in Practice*, **10** (3), 225–40.

Calder, M. & Hackett, S. (eds) (2003) *Assessment in Child Care*. Russell House Publishing, Lyme Regis.

Cantrill, P. (2006) *Overview of the 'W' Family*. Sheffield Area Child Protection Committee, Sheffield.

Channer, Y. & Parton, P. (1990) Racism, cultural relativism and child protection. In: *Violence against Children Study Group. Taking Child Abuse Seriously*, pp. 105–20. Unwin, London and New York.

Chasnoff, I.J. & Lowder, L. (1999) Prenatal alcohol and drug use and risk for child maltreatment. In: *Neglected Children, Research, Practice and Policy* (ed. H. Dubowitz), pp. 132–55. Sage, London.

Christensen, E. (1997) Aspects of a preventative approach to support children of alcoholics. *Child Abuse Review*, **6** (1), 24–34.

Cleaver, H., Unell, I. & Aldgate, J. (1999) *Children's Needs – Parenting Capacity*. The Stationery Office, London.

Coohey, C. (1995) Neglectful mothers, their mothers and partners: the significance of mutual aid. *Child Abuse and Neglect*, **19** (8), 885–95.

Cooper, A. (2005) Surface and depth in the Victoria Climbié report. *Child and Family Social Work*, **10** (1), 1–10.

Cooper, C. (1985) 'Good enough', borderline and 'bad enough' parenting. In: *Good Enough Parenting* (eds M. Adcock & R. White), pp. 58–80. British Agencies for Adoption and Fostering, London.

Creighton, S. (1986) *NSPCC Research Briefing*, No. 5, August. NSPCC, London.

Crittenden, P. (1988) Family dyadic patterns of functioning in maltreating families. In: *Early Predicting and Prevention of Child Abuse* (eds K. Browne, C. Davies & P. Strattan), pp. 161–89. Wiley, London and New York.

Crittenden, P. (1993) An information processing perspective on the behaviour of neglectful parents. *Criminal Justice and Behaviour*, **20** (1), 27–48.

Crittenden, P.M. (1999) Child neglect: causes and contributors. In: *Neglected Children. Research, Practice and Policy* (ed. H. Dubowitz), pp. 47–68. Sage, California.

Crouch, J. & Milner, J. (1993) Effects of child neglect on children. *Criminal Justice and Behaviour*, **20** (1), 49–65.

Daniel, B. & Taylor, J. (2005) Do they care? The role of fathers in cases of child neglect. In: *Child Neglect: Practice Issues for Health and Social Care* (eds B. Daniel & J. Taylor), pp. 263–78. Jessica Kingsley, London.

Daniel, B., Wassell, S. & Gilligan, R. (1999) *Child Development for Child Care and Protection Workers*. Jessica Kingsley, London.

Darlington, Y., Feeney, J. & Rixon, K. (2005) Practice challenges at the intersection of child protection and mental health. *Child and Family Social Work*, **10** (3), 239–48.

Davies, M. (2002) A few thoughts about the mind, the brain and a child with early deprivation. *Journal of Analytical Psychology*, **4**, 421–35.

Department for Education and Skills (2004) *Every Child Matters*. Stationery Office, London.

Department for Education and Skills (2005a) *Referrals, Assessments and Children and Young People on Child Protection Registers*. National Statistics. Department for Education and Skills, London.

Department for Education and Skills (2005b) *Early Impacts of Sure Start Local Programmes on Children and Families*. Department for Education and Skills, London.

Department for Education and Skills (2006a) *Working Together to Safeguard Children*. Stationery Office, London.

Department for Education and Skills (2006b) Boarding school plan for vulnerable children. *Times Ed. Supplement*, 6 November. Department for Education and Skills, London.

Department of Health (1988) *Protecting Children: a Guide for Social Workers Undertaking a Comprehensive Assessment*. HMSO, London.

Department of Health (1989) *Working Together*. HMSO, London.

Department of Health (1995) *Child Protection Messages from Research. Studies in Child Protection*. HMSO, London.

Department of Health (1999) *Framework for the Assessment of Children*. HMSO, London.

Department of Health (2000a) *Framework for the Assessment of Children in Need and Their Families. The Assessment Framework*. The Stationery Office, London.

Department of Health (2000b) *Framework for the Assessment of Children in Need and Their Families. Practice Guidance*. The Stationery Office, London.

Department of Health (2000c) *Framework for the Assessment of Children in Need and Their Families. Questionnaires and Scales*. The Stationery Office, London.

Department of Health and Social Security (1974a) *Report of Committee of Inquiry into Care and Supervision Provided in Relation to Maria Colwell*. HMSO, London.

Department of Health and Social Security (1974b) *Non-accidental Injury to Children*. LASSL (73) 14. DHSS, London.

Department of Work and Pensions (2003) *Households Below Average Income 2001–2*. The Stationery Office, London.

Dickens, J. (1993) Assessment and the control of social work: an analysis of reasons for the non-use of the child assessment order. *Journal of Social Welfare and Family Law*, **15** (2), 88–100.

Dickens, J. (2006) Care, control and change in child care protection proceedings: dilemmas for social workers, managers and lawyers. *Child and Family Social Work*, **11** (1), 23–32.

Dickens, J (forthcoming 2007) Child neglect and the law: catapults, thresholds and delay. *Child Abuse Review*.

Donaldson, T. (2004) *The changing face of care under the children (NI) order, 1995: a prospective study of decision making and care*. Unpublished thesis, Queens University, Belfast.

Dube, S.R., Anda, R.F., Felitti, V.J., Croft, J.B., Edwards, V.J. & Giles, W.H. (2001) Growing up with parental alcohol abuse: exposure to childhood abuse, neglect, and household dysfunction. *Child Abuse and Neglect*, **25** (12), 1627–40.

Dubowitz, H. (1999) *Neglected Children. Research, Practice and Policy*. Sage, California.

Dunn, J. & Plomin, R. (1990) *Separate Lives. Why Siblings are so Different*. Basic Books, New York.

Dunn, M., Tarta, R., Mezzick, A., Vanukov. M., Kirisci, L. & Kirilova, A. (2002) Origins and consequences of neglect in substance abuse families. *Clinical Psychological Review*, **22** (5), 1063–90.

Dutt, R. & Phillips, M. (1996) Race, culture and the prevention of child abuse. In submission to Commission of Inquiry into the prevention of child abuse. *Childhood Matters*, **2**, 154–96.

Dutt, R. & Phillips, M. (2000) Assessing black children in need and their families. In: *Department of Health Framework for the Assessment of Children in Need and Their Families*. The Stationery Office, London.

Egeland, B. (1988a) The consequences of physical and emotional neglect on the development of young children. *Research Symposium on Child Neglect*. Washington, DC.

Egeland, B. (1988b) Breaking the cycle of abuse: implications for prediction and intervention. In: *Early Prediction and Prevention of Child Abuse* (eds K. Browne, H. Hanks, P. Stratton & C. Hamilton). John Wiley, London and New York.

Egeland, B. & Sroufe, A. (1981) Developmental sequelae of maltreatment in infancy. In: *New Directions for Child Development* (eds R. Rizley & D. Cicchetti), pp. 77–92. Jossey Bass, San Francisco.

Egeland, B., Sroufe, A. & Erikson, M. (1983) The developmental consequences of different patterns of maltreatment. *Child Abuse and Neglect*, **7**, 459–69.

Emerson, E., Malam, S., Davies, I. & Spencer, K. (2005) *Adults with Learning Difficulties in England*. www.ic.nhs.uk/pubs/learndiff2004

Farmer, E. & Owen, M. (1995) *Child Protection Practice: Private Risks and Public Remedies*. HMSO, London.

Featherstone, B. (1999) Taking mothers seriously. *Child and Family Social Work*, **4** (1), 43–54.

Featherstone, B. (2001) Putting fathers on the child welfare agenda. *Child and Family Social Work*, **6** (2), 179–86.

Finch, J. (1989) *Family Obligations and Social Change*. Cambridge Policy Press, London.

Fonagy, P., Steele, M., Steele, H., Higgit, A. & Target, M. (1994) The theory and practice of resilience. *Journal of Child Psychology and Psychiatry*, **35** (2), 231–57.

Fox, L., Long, S. & Langlois, A. (1988) Patterns of language comprehension deficit in abused and neglected children. *Journal of Speech and Hearing Disorders*, **53**, 239–44.

Fox, S. & Dingwall, R. (1988) An exploratory study of variations in social workers' and health visitors' definitions of child maltreatment. *British Journal of Social Work*, **5** (5), 467–77.

Freeman, P. & Ingham, J. (2006) Multiple child abuse that involves wider kin and family friends within intergenerational networks: a theoretical model. In: *Assessment in Kinship Care* (eds C. Talbot & M. Calder), pp. 87–98. Russell House, Lyme Regis.

Frost, N., Johnston, E., Stein, M. & Wallis, L. (1997) *Negotiated Friendship*. Home Start, Leicester.

Frost, N., Robinson, M. & Aming, A. (2005) Social workers in multidisciplinary teams: issues and dilemmas for professional practice. *Child and Family Social Work*, **10** (3), 187–96.

Fuller, R. & Stevenson, O. (1983) *Policies, Programmes and Disadvantage. A Review of Literature*. Heinemann, London.

Garbarino, J. & Collins, C.C. (1999) Child neglect: the family with a hole in the middle. In: *Neglected Children. Research, Practice and Policy* (ed. H. Dubowitz), pp. 1–23. Sage Publications, London.

Gaudin, J. (1993) *Child Neglect: A Guide for Intervention*. National Center on Child Abuse and Neglect (US Department of Health and Human Services), Washington, DC.

Ghate, D. & Hazel, N. (2002) *Parenting in Poor Environments*. Policy Research Bureau. Jessica Kingsley, London.

Glaser, D., Prior, V. & Lynch, M. (1997) Is the term child protection applicable to emotional abuse? *Child Abuse Review*, **6** (31), 5–29.

Goldson, B. (2006) Child protection and the 'Juvenile Secure Estate' in England and Wales: controversies, complexities and concerns. In: *Youth Justice and Child Protection* (eds M. Hill, A. Lockyer & F. Stone), pp. 104–20. Jessica Kingsley, London.

Goldstein, J., Solnit, A., Goldstein, S. & Freud, A. (1996) *The Best Interests of the Child*. The Free Press, New York.

Goodringe, S. (2000) *A Jigsaw of Services: Inspection of Services to Support Disabled Adults in their Parenting Role*. Department of Health, London.

Gough, D. (1993) The case for and against prevention. In: *Child Abuse and Child Abusers* (Research Highlights in Social Work 24) (ed. L. Waterhouse), pp. 208–52.

Government response to 'Hidden Harm' (2005) DfES, London.

Hackett, L. & Hackett, R. (1994) Child rearing practices and psychiatric disorder in Gujarati and British children. *British Journal of Social Work*, **24**, 191–202.

Hallett, C. (1995) *Interagency Coordination in Child Protection*. HMSO, London.

Hallett, C. & Stevenson, O. (1980) *Child Abuse: Aspects of Interprofessional Cooperation*. Allen & Unwin, London.

Hardin, G. (1980) The tragedy of the commons. In: *Economics, Ecology and Ethics. Essays Towards a Steady State Economy* (ed. H. Daly), pp. 100–114. Freeman, New York.

Hill, M., Lockyer, A. & Stone, F. (eds) (2006) *Youth Justice and Child Protection*. Jessica Kingsley, London.

Home Office (1950) *Children Neglected or Ill-treated in Their Own Homes*. HMSO, London.

Home Office (2004) *Young People, Crime and Anti-social Behaviour*. Research and Statistics Directorate, London.

Home Start (2004) *Annual Report*. Home Start, London.

Home Start (2005) *Annual Report*. Home Start, London.

Horton, C. (ed.) (2005) *Working with Children 2006–2007. Facts, Figures and Information*. Society Guardian & Sage Publishing, NCH, the Children's Charity, London.

Howe, D. (1996) Child abuse and the bureaucratisation of social work. *Sociological Review*, **38**, 491–508.

Howe, D. (1997) *Patterns of Adoption*. Blackwell Science, Oxford.

Howe, D. (2005) *Child Abuse and Neglect*. Palgrave McMillan, Basingstoke.

Iwaniec, D. (1995) *The Emotionally Abused and Neglected Child*. John Wiley, Chichester.

Iwaniec, D., Donaldson, T. & Allweis, M. (2004) The plight of neglected children – social work and judicial decision making and management of neglect cases. *Child and Family Law Quarterly*, **16** (4), 423–36.

Jack, J. (2000) Ecological influences in parenting and child development. *British Journal of Social Work*, **30** (6), 708–20.

Jehu, D., Yelloly, M. & Shaw, M. (1972) *Behaviour Modification in Social Work*. Wiley and Sons, London and New York.

Jones, J. & McNeely, M. (1980) Mothers who neglect and those who do not: a comparative study. *Journal of Contemporary Social Work*, 424–31.

Journal of Intergenerational Relations: Programs, Policy and Research. (2003) The Howarth Press, Inc., New York.

Jung, C.G. (1993) *Collected Works*, Volume 16. Routledge, London.

Kanter, J. (ed.) (2004) *Face to Face with Children*. Karnac, London.

Kempe, C. & Helfer, R. (1968) *The Battered Child*. Chicago University Press, Chicago.

Korbin, J. (1991) Cross-cultural perspectives and research directions for the twenty-first century. *Child Abuse and Neglect*, **15** (Suppl. 1), 67–77.

Korbin, J. & Spilsbury, J. (1999) Cultural competence and child neglect. In: *Neglected Children; Research, Practice and Policy* (ed. H. Dubowitz), pp. 69–88. Sage, London.

Kurtz, P., Gaudin, J., Wordaski, J. & Howing, P. (1993a) Maltreatment and the school-aged child: school performance consequences. *Child Abuse and Neglect*, **17**, 581–9.

Kurtz, P., Gaudin, J., Howing, P. & Wodarski, J. (1993b) The consequences of physical abuse and neglect on the school-age child. *Children and Youth Services Review*, **15**, 85–104.

Laming, H. (2003) *Inquiry into the Death of Victoria Climbié*. Stationery Office, London.

Lavery, R. (1996) The child assessment order – a reassessment. *Child and Family Law Quarterly*, **8** (1), 41–56.

Llewellyn, G. & McConnell, D. (2002) Mothers with learning disabilities and their support networks. *Journal of Intellectual Disability Research*, **46** (part 1), 17–38.

London Borough of Lambeth (1987) *Whose Child? The Report of the Panel of Inquiry into the Death of Tyra Henry*. London Borough of Lambeth, London.

Lord Chancellor's Department (2005) *Protocol for Judicial Case Management in Public Law Children Act Cases*. LCD, London.

Lynch, M. & Stevenson, O. (1990) *Fox, Stephanie: Report of the Practice Review*. Commissioned by the Wandsworth Child Protection Committee, Wandsworth.

McConnell, D. & Llewellyn, G. (2002) Stereotypes, parents with intellectual disability and child protection. *Journal of Social Welfare and Family Law*, **24** (3), 297–317.

MacDonald, G. (2001) *Effective Intervention for Child Abuse and Neglect*. Wiley & Sons, Chichester.

McGaw, S. (1997) Practical support for parents with learning disabilities. In: *Adults with Learning Disabilities* (eds P. O'Hara & A. Sperlinger). Wiley & Sons, Chichester.

McGaw, S. & Sturmey, P. (1994) Assessing parents with learning disabilities: the parental skills model. *Child Abuse Review*, **3** (1), 27–35.

McGlone, F., Park, A. & Roberts, C. (1996) Relative values: kinship and friendship. *British Social Attitudes*: 13th Report, pp. 53–72. Dartmouth Publishing Company, Dartmouth.

Maitra, B. (1995) Giving due consideration to the family's racial and cultural background. In: *Assessment of Parenting* (eds P. Reder & C. Lucey), pp. 151–68. Routledge, London and New York.

Marsh, P. & Crow, G. (1997) *Family Group Conferences*. Blackwell Science Ltd, Oxford.

Mass, M. (1996) The narrative of parents. *Journal of the Theory of Social Behaviour*, **26** (4), 423–42.

Mattinson, J. & Sinclair, I. (1979) *Mate and Stalemate*. Blackwell Publishers, Oxford.

Middleton, S. (2006) *The Social Fund. Current Role and Future Directions*. Joseph Rowntree Foundation, York.

Minty, B. & Pattinson, G. (1994) The nature of child neglect. *British Journal of Social Work*, **24**, 733–48.

Murphy, H. & Harbin, F. (2003) The assessment of parental substance misuse and its impact on child care. In: *Assessment in Child Care* (eds M.C. Calder & S. Hackett), pp. 353–61. Russell House Publishing, Lyme Regis.

Murphy, J.M., Jellinek, M., Quinn, D., Smith, G., Poitrast, F.G. & Goshko, M. (1991) Substance abuse and serious child mistreatment: prevalence, risk, and outcome in a court sample. *Child Abuse and Neglect*, **15**, 197–211.

National Clearinghouse on Child Neglect and Abuse (2001) *Information Review. Understanding the Effects of Maltreatment on Early Brain Development*. National Clearinghouse on Child Abuse and Neglect, Washington, DC.

Ney, P., Fung, T. & Wickett, A. (1994) The worst combination of child abuse and neglect. *Child Abuse and Neglect*, **18** (9), 705–14.

O'Hagan, K. (1999) Culture, cultural identity and cultural sensitivity in child and family social work. *Child and Family Social Work*, **4** (4), 269–81.

Olsen, R. & Wates, M. (2003) *Disabled Parents: Examining Research Assumptions*. Research and Practice, Darlington.

Owusa-Bempah, K. (1998) The relevance of confidentiality in social work practice across two cultures. In: *Social Work Processes* (eds B. Compton & B. Galaway), 5th edn. Brooks Cole, Pacific Grove, California.

Owusa-Bempah, K. & Howitt, M. (1997) Socio-genealogical connections, attachment theory and child care practice. *Child and Family Social Work*, **2** (4), 199–208.

Parton, N. (1985) *The Politics of Child Abuse*. Macmillan, London and New York.

Pearce, J. (2003) Parental mental health and child protection – making the links through training. *Child Abuse Review,* **12**, 114–118.

Perry, B. (1996) *Neurodevelopmental Adaptation to Violence.* http:www.childtrauma. org/CMMATERIALS/vortex_interd.asp

Philp, F. (1963) *Family Failure.* Faber and Faber, London.

Pianti, R., Egeland, B. & Erikson, M. (1989) The antecedents of maltreatment. In: *Child Maltreatment* (eds D. Cicchetti & V. Carlson). Cambridge University Press, Cambridge.

Platt, S., Martin, C., & Hunt, S. (1989) Damp housing, mould growth and symptomatic health state. *British Medical Journal,* **298**, 1673–8.

Polansky, N., Ammons, P. & Gaudin, J. (1985a) Loneliness and isolation in child neglect. *Social Casework,* 38–48.

Polansky, N., Gaudin, J., Ammons, P. & Davis, K. (1985b) The psychological ecology of the neglectful mother. *Child Abuse and Neglect,* **9**, 265–75.

Prior, V. & Glaser, D. (2006) *Understanding Attachment and Attachment Disorders.* Jessica Kingsley, London.

Rashid, S. (1996) Attachment viewed through a cultural lens. In: *Attachment and Loss in Child and Family Social Work* (ed. D. Howe), pp. 59–81. Avebury, Basingstoke.

Reder, P. & Duncan, S. (2003) Understanding communication in child protection networks. *Child Abuse Review,* **12**, 82–100.

Robertson, J. & Robertson, J. (1953) *A Two-year-old Goes to Hospital* (film). Ipswich Concord Films Council, Ipswich.

Robertson, J. & Robertson, J. (1969) *John: 17 Months: Nine Days at a Residential Nursery* (film). Ipswich Concord Films Council, Ipswich.

Rutter, M. & Madge, N. (1976) *Cycles of Disadvantage: a Review of Research.* Longman, London.

Rutter, M. & Rutter, M. (1993) *Developing Minds: Challenge and Continuity Across the Life Span.* Penguin Books, Harmondsworth.

Rutter, M., Anderson Wood, L., Beckett, C., Bredenkamp, D., Castle, J., Groothues, C., Kreppner, J., Keaveney, L., Lord, C., O'Connor, T. and the English and Romanian Study Team. (1999) Quasi-autistic patterns following severe early global privation. *Journal of Child Psychology and Psychiatry,* **40** (4), 537–49.

Ryan, M. & Little, M. (2000) *Working with Families.* HMSO, London.

Seagull, E. (1987) Social support and child maltreatment: a review of the evidence. *Child Abuse and Neglect,* **11**, 41–52.

Seligman, M. (1975) *Helplessness: On Depression, Development and Death.* Freeman, San Francisco.

Sheppard, M. (1997) Double jeopardy: the link between child abuse and maternal depression. *Child and Family Social Work,* **2** (2), 91–108.

Shore, R. (1997) *Rethinking the Brain. Families Work.* NY Institute, New York.

Skuse, D.H. (1985) Non-organic failure to thrive: a reappraisal. *Archives of Diseases in Childhood,* **20**, 173–8.

Spencer, N. & Baldwin, N. (2005) Economic, cultural and social contexts of neglect. In: *Practice Issues for Health and Social Care* (eds J. Taylor & B. Daniel), pp. 26–42. Jessica Kingsley, London.

Stanley, N., Penhale, B., Riordan, D., Barbour, R. & Holden, S. (2003) *Child Protection and Mental Health Services*. The Policy Press, Bristol.

Stevenson, O. (1989) Multidisciplinary work in child protection. In: *Child Abuse, Public Policy and Professional Practice* (ed. O. Stevenson), pp. 173–203. Harvester Wheatsheaf, London.

Stevenson, O. (1996) Emotional abuse and neglect: a time for reappraisal. *Child and Family Social Work*, **1** (1), 13–18.

Stevenson, O. (1999) Children in need and abused: interprofessional and inter-agency responses. In: *Child Welfare in the UK* (ed. O. Stevenson), pp. 100–120. Blackwell Science, Oxford.

Stevenson, O. (2005a) Genericism and specialisation. The story since 1970. *British Journal of Social Work*, **35** (5), 569–86.

Stevenson, O. (2005b) Working Together in Cases of Neglect: Key Issues. In: *Child Neglect* (eds J. Taylor & B. Daniel), pp. 97–112. Jessica Kingsley, London.

Talbot, C. & Calder, M. (2006) *Assessment in Kinship Care*. Russell House, Lyme Regis.

Tanner, K. & Turney, D. (2003) What do we know about child neglect? A critical review of the literature and its application to social work practice. *Child and Family Social Work*, **8** (1), 25–35.

Tanner, K. & Turney, D. (2006) *Understanding and Working with Neglect*. No. 10. Research and Practice Briefings, Nottingham. www.rip.org.uk/publications/researchbriefings.asp

Tarleton, B., Ward, L. & Howarth, J. (2006) *Finding the Right Support*. Norah Fry Research Centre, The Baring Foundation, Bristol. www.bris.ac.uk/depts/norahfry

Taylor, A. & Kroll, B. (2004) Working with parental substance misuse: dilemmas for practice. *British Journal of Social Work*, **34**, 1115–32.

Taylor, J. & Daniel, B. (2005) Do they care? The role of fathers in cases of child care. In: *Child Neglect: Practice Issues for Health and Social Care* (eds B. Daniel & J. Taylor), pp. 263–78. Jessica Kingsley, London.

The Bridge Consultancy (1995) *Paul: Death Through Neglect*. The Bridge Consultancy Services, London.

Thoburn, J., Lewis, A. & Shemmings, D. (1995) *Paternalism or Partnership? Family Involvement in the Child Protection Process*. HMSO, London.

Thoburn, J., Wilding, J. & Watson, J. (2000) *Family Support in Cases of Emotional Maltreatment and Neglect*. The Stationery Office, London.

Townsend, P., Davidson, N. & Whitehead, M. (1988) *Inequalities in Health*. Penguin Books, London.

Tresider. J., Jones, J. & Glennie, S. (2003) *Report of a Multi-agency Action Research Project to Improve Service Delivery to Families with Complex Needs*. University of Nottingham, Nottingham.

Trowell, J. & Bower, M. (1995) *The Emotional Needs of Young Children and Their Families.* Routledge, London and New York.

Tunstill, J., Aldgate, J. & Hughes, M. (2007) *Improving Children's Services Networks. Lessons from Family Centres.* Jessica Kingsley, London.

Turney, D. (2005) Who cares? The role of mothers in child neglect. In: *Child Neglect: Practice Issues for Health and Social Care* (eds B. Daniel & J. Taylor), pp. 249–62. Jessica Kingsley, London.

Unicef (2000) *A League Table of Child Poverty in Rich Nations.* Unicef, Geneva.

Walker, M. & Glasgow, M. (2005) Parental substance misuse and the implications for children. Lessons from research and practice in one centre. In: *Child Neglect: Practice Issues for Health and Social Care* (eds B. Daniel & J. Taylor), pp. 206–27. Jessica Kingsley, London.

Werner, E. (1990) Protective factors and individual resilience. In: *Handbook of Early Childhood Intervention* (eds S. Meisels & J. Shonkoff), pp. 97–116. Cambridge University Press, Cambridge.

Winnicott, C. (2004) Communicating with children. In: *Face to Face with Children* (ed. J. Kanter), pp. 184–97. Karnac, London.

Youell, B. (2005) Observation in social work practice. In: *Psychoanalytic Theory for Social Work Practice* (ed. M. Bower), pp. 47–58. Routledge, Abingdon.

Young, S. (2006) Kinship placement and parents with intellectual disabilities. In: *Assessment in Kinship Care* (eds C. Talbot & M. Calder), pp. 57–66. Russell House, Lyme Regis.

Youth Justice Board (2004) *Sustaining the Success: Extending the Guidance.* Youth Justice Board, London.

Zuravin, S. & Diblasio, P. (1996) The correlates of child physical abuse and neglect by delinquent mothers. *Journal of Family Violence,* **11**, 149–160.

Zuravin, S.J. (1999) Child neglect: a review of deprivation and measurement research. In: *Neglected Children* (ed. H. Dubovitz), pp. 24–46 Research, Practice and Policy, Sage, California.

Index